CYCLING THE RIVER LOIRE
THE WAY OF ST MARTIN

ABOUT THE AUTHOR

John Higginson has been a long-distance fell walker for many years. Having been a keen cyclist in his youth, he took up long-distance cycling in Europe a few years after he retired from the post of headmaster of a Cheshire primary school. He is now a writer and lecturer.

He and his wife, Andrea, who have ridden both south to north and east to west across France, the length of the medieval pilgrimage route from Le Puy-en-Velay in France to Santiago de Compostela in north-west Spain, and the Danube Cycleway from Donaueschingen to Budapest, spent many years touring in the Loire valley before embarking on this book which describes the route and its myriad places of interest.

John Higginson has also written *The Way of St James – A Cyclist's Guide* (Cicerone, 2005) and *The Danube Cycleway – Donaueschingen to Budapest* (Cicerone, 2003).

CYCLING THE RIVER LOIRE
THE WAY OF ST MARTIN

by
John Higginson

photographs by Andrea Higginson

2 POLICE SQUARE, MILNTHORPE, CUMBRIA LA7 7PY
www.cicerone.co.uk

© John Higginson 2003
Reprinted 2009 (with updates)

ISBN-13: 978 1 85284 383 0
ISBN-10: 1 85284 383 7

A catalogue record for this book is available from the British Library.

DEDICATION

With thanks to Andrea for thirty-five years of adventure

Front cover: Château de la Roche below St. Paul de Vezelin

CONTENTS

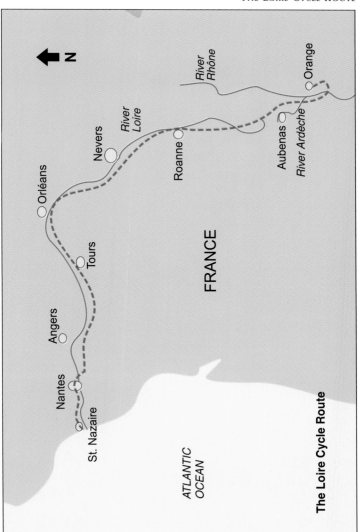

The Loire Cycle Route

The approach to Gien

INTRODUCTION

The River Loire is known as the Queen of Rivers in France, and for most Europeans this beautiful waterway carries the same title. This is probably as a result of the magnificent châteaux built along its banks between Nevers and Angers, but there is far more to the Loire than a series of ostentatious pleasure domes.

For nature lovers, the region between the Loire's source high in the Massif Central and the end of the Loire gorge near Roanne is unforgettable. It teems with both flora and fauna. It is possible to spend days here kayaking between vertical cliffs. For boating enthusiasts, the central section, accompanied by canals and waterways, is an area of outstanding interest including an abundance of industrial archaeology; and for lovers of fine wine, the Loire produces vineyard after vineyard of the world's greatest vintages. For cyclists, however, the River Loire offers one of the finest long-distance rides in Europe.

This is no suffocating cycle-way denying cyclists access to villages and towns because they might meet vehicular traffic. Instead, the Loire has a natural accompaniment of country lanes and minor roads which hug its banks and provide easy access to every place which takes the cyclist's fancy. In fact, it is the tiny gems discovered along the way which make this journey so fasci-nating. They will lead those interested from prehistoric and Gallo-Roman remains close to the river's source through every phase of the history of France down to views of the future in the shipyards at its mouth.

Any journey along the Loire will become intertwined with the story of Saint Martin (see box p.11). The majority of churches along the route are dedicated to him, and the river passes by both his home and his final resting place. It even provided the means of transport between the two.

This is, indeed, a river and a cycle route for everyone.

BACKGROUND

The Loire first sees the light of day as it bubbles out of the foot of a large volcanic plug high in the Massif Central. Le Gerbier de Jonc has five springs, each making its claim to be the source of the Loire, but within a hundred metres they all join together

One source of the River Loire at Le Gerbier de Jonc, Stage 5

The broadening Loire below Ste. Eulalie, Stage 6

to form a recognisable stream which flows lazily into the Atlantic over 1300km away. The river valley between these points forms the route described in this book. From its source to Orléans it travels in a northerly direction, but then the Loire turns a right-angle bend, swinging to the west until it reaches the sea.

From its source to the city of Le Puy en Velay, the Loire is very much a mountain river, occasionally dammed, plunging between volcanic rocks or spreading into long lakes behind massive barrages. The winding country roads which accompany it climb and fall erratically, sometimes crossing it on narrow bridges, sometimes leaving it to negotiate a mountain col before returning to its banks. On this section of its length there is never a dull moment, although it is possible to cycle all day on these roads and never see a single car!

Between Le Puy and Roanne, the river continues to flow in a series of gorges, but these are less wild, with good roads running alongside. There are now numerous towns and villages, many with castles and colourful histories. The way is still hilly but less rugged.

North of Roanne, the whole nature of the river changes. Its valley widens and the landscape is dominated by agriculture. Towns and cities are well scattered, but farming villages abound. There are far more cattle than people, and the river flows lazily alongside man-made waterways. The riding along this stretch of the route is easy if a little less inspiring.

West of Orléans the ways become much busier. The tourist industry,

Saint Martin (316–397AD)

Martin, the son of a Roman army officer, was born in the year 316 in what is now Hungary. As a boy, he moved to Italy and was educated in Pavia in the north of the country. In 331, against his will, he was drafted into the Roman army, serving in Gaul (present day France).

Whilst garrisoned in Amiens in 337, Martin came across a naked, starving beggar. Contrary to all the laws of Rome, he defaced his uniform by cutting his military cloak in two and handing half to the beggar before proclaiming himself to be a soldier of Christ. Shortly afterwards, Martin was baptised into the Christian Church.

The pilgrimage town of Candes St. Martin, Stage 19

He asked for a discharge from the Roman army but was accused of cowardice. It is said that to prove his bravery he stood, unarmed, in the battle line holding only a cross. The enemy fled, terrified. Soon afterwards he was granted his discharge.

Martin became a disciple of St Hilary of Poitiers in 339, travelling widely in Europe before founding the first French monastery at Ligugé. He was invited, at the age of fifty-six, to become bishop of Tours, and although reluctant to take on the responsibility – he preferred to live the monastic life, still inhabiting a cell near the church – he served the diocese for twenty-five years. He was a dedicated missionary, promoting his faith by example. On his journeys he is said to have healed lepers and raised a man from the dead.

On his death in November 397, his body was floated from Candes to Tours for burial. Over 800 of his followers are said to have accompanied his coffin, and as his lifeless body floated along the Loire, it is said that the plants along the river's bank, despite it being November, burst into flower. This phenomenon still occurs occasionally today when climatic conditions are favourable and is known as a Saint Martin's Winter.

Each year on his feast day, November 11th, crowds of pilgrims descend on his burial place in the Basilica at Tours to pay their respects and to celebrate the life of this great French saint.

Boats on the Canal de Roanne à Digoin near Briennon, Stage 10

PREPARATION

To reap the maximum enjoyment from this journey it is worth putting in a certain amount of preparation. The journey is, at times, fairly demanding both physically and intellectually, and a knowledgeable, well-prepared cyclist will enjoy the cycle route along the River Loire so much more.

Cycles

In its early stages this route is fairly demanding, and so some issues about the type of bike and equipment for the journey need to be considered. There are also long, level sections which, if wind-assisted, could afford some high-speed travelling. In either case, a set of seven gears (11–26) on a triple chain ring (42/32/22) will provide all the assistance needed for this journey.

Most cyclists encountered along

based on the mighty châteaux of the Loire, comes to the fore with many roads full of holiday traffic. However, it is always possible to find narrow, unused lanes, often on the very banks of the river, to avoid the crush. The Loire Cycle Way, which appears occasionally in this section, can be of some limited help but is not, as yet, reliable enough to be followed slavishly.

The final section of this ride proves both surprising and fascinating. From Angers to St. Nazaire, the route becomes hilly again, with a spectacular length of riding high above the river along the Angevine Corniche and through the vineyards of Anjou before descending, after Nantes, to meander through the sluggish countryside of the Audubon Marais.

Running repairs in Cosne Cours sur Loire, Stage 14

the way will be local club riders out for a day's spin. They will pass tourists with a wave and a shout as they disappear for ever. It is then necessary to remind oneself that they are not carrying everything necessary for a month's journey!

There are almost no off-road sections along this route, although a few of the country lanes and cycleways within an 80km radius of Orléans have surfaces which leave much to be desired. My wife and I used American Trek multi-track bikes. Anything similar will cope with these conditions. Panaracer Pasela kevlar tyres again gave trouble-free rolling with not a single puncture on either bike.

Straight handlebars with bar ends set to give an alternative hand grip ease the strain on tired backs but can still cause numbness of hands after a lengthy stretch. The choice between straight and 'drop' handlebars, where gear changing is less easy, is yours. A truly comfortable riding position is more important, as this will prevent stiffness and soreness as the journey progresses.

Equipment

Weather conditions can be extreme if this journey is undertaken in anything but the summer months. The Massif Central (a home of Nordic skiing) can produce plummeting temperatures, torrential rain and gale force winds at any time of the year, and this should be borne in mind when planning equipment.

The author and a large bottle of Montlouis, Stage 18

A pair of totally waterproof panniers and a similar bar bag and map holder are essential. There is nothing worse than arriving at a destination to find that everything in your bags is soaking wet and your only map has disintegrated. Totally waterproof bags are expensive, but for this sort of journey they are worth the outlay. Contrary to popular myth, condensation does not form inside them unless damp clothes are carried inside. 'Start dry and stay dry' is the motto for long-distance cyclists the world over. Similarly, lightweight, breathable, waterproof clothing which does not become clammy and cold after several hours' continuous cycling is a must, as is something light but warm to wear in the evenings when, in the mountains, temperatures drop dramatically. For long-distance cyclists anywhere, comfortable padded cycling shorts are essential for day-on-day riding.

In the Massif Central, when travelling high above precipitous sides of the river in rain and gusty winds, wearing a cape is not a wise decision. Whilst capes do allow the wind to pass over the body, keeping it dry, their propensity to act as a sail makes them too dangerous to seriously contemplate on this journey. A waterproof, quick-drying jacket is a far more sensible choice. Padded gloves, too, make life more comfortable when riding on worn, rutted tarmac.

Flies and midges can be a severe problem, particularly in summer, on this route. Whilst cycling, a pair of tight-fitting glasses should keep eyes protected, and in the evening either mosquito repellent or a net should ensure a good night's sleep.

Maps

There is no doubt that an inappropriate set of maps for a touring holiday can prove disastrous if not even dangerous. (I once met a walker trying to navigate his way up Great Gable using a motorist's road atlas!) There should be no such problem when cycling around France.

The perfect cyclist's map is the Institut Geographique National (IGN), Serie Verte, scale 1:100,000 (1cm = 1km). Michelin produce a 1:200,000 series, but whilst these are good for route planning, they do not show sufficient detail for the discerning cyclist.

The cathedral cloisters in Le Puy, Stage 7

The only drawback to the IGN maps is that a large number of them are needed for a journey such as this. To progressively reduce the load, it is suggested that they be posted home once they are no longer needed. The sketch maps in this book are sufficient to give an indication of the route but cannot show a true picture of the surrounding landscape.

The IGN maps used on this journey are No. 59 (Privas/Alès), No. 50 (St. Étienne/Le Puy-en-Velay), No. 43 (Lyon/Vichy), No. 36 (Nevers/ Autun), No. 27 (Orléans/la Charité-sur-Loire), No. 26 (Orléans/Tours), No. 5 (Angers/ Chinon) and No. 24 (Nantes/ Châteaubriant). All these are available from good bookshops in the UK and can be found in Les Maisons de la Presse in most small towns in France.

Town plans are readily available, usually free of charge, at tourist offices, and these often include lists of accommodation as well as places of interest worth visiting.

Fitness

This is a long ride and some training should be considered before embarking on it. My wife and I are fast approaching sixty, yet we only embarked on light training (20 km per day) a month before we left England and had no serious difficulty in completing the journey. The secret, if time allows, is not to ride further than is necessary in a day – this is where careful study of the maps is essential. Be prepared to stop and admire the view or wander round a village on foot instead of in the saddle. Bars and cafés are there to rest in as well as drink in. Proprietors in France will never shoo you out.

The first quarter of the journey does entail some serious hill climbing. Many roads are steep, and the climb to the source of the Loire is very, very long (39km). However, if regular rests are taken, there is nothing to daunt a reasonably fit cyclist.

The central section of the route is flat, easy cycling, but it is tempting to ride extra long distances in this area and this can prove just as exhausting as climbing hills. Once again, plan your route carefully and remember that the following morning another long ride will be in prospect. It is in this part of the ride that a truly comfortable riding position is essential.

The final part of this journey is surprisingly hilly and, as at all stages on this ride, it is better to measure your day in time rather than distance. Remember, the longer your day, the less enthusiastic you may be to ride the next.

Accommodation

Much of this journey is away from tourist areas and, consequently, overnight accommodation may be sparse. However, it is highly unlikely that you will have nowhere to rest your head for the night. Wherever you consider, ask to see the room – and if it is not what you want, say so. The French expect this. Also check that there is somewhere safe to store the bikes. They are just as important as you are.

There is only a handful of *gîtes d'étape* available along this route, but where they exist it is advisable to use them. They are the French equivalent of a superior youth hostel, often with dormitory accommodation, but they provide full kitchen and washing facilities and charge very little. Some even provide breakfast and evening meals.

Chambres d'hôtes, similar to an English bed and breakfast, are becoming more commonplace. They are usually very comfortable with genial hosts. Some also offer evening meals. However, the cost of these establishments varies dramatically and it is always best to check the price before committing oneself. It is worth remembering that few hosts speak any English, and at least a

Old and new transport in St. Just–St. Rambert, Stage 9

smattering of French will make all the difference to the enjoyment of staying in such places.

In recent years, hotels in France have become a very economical form of overnight accommodation. Nearly all now offer en suite facilities. Breakfast, which can be expensive, is an optional extra and there is always somewhere to store bikes safely. If you are not too bothered about the location of the hotel, look for those near railway and bus stations. They are invariably cheap and often provide evening meals at surprisingly low prices. Remember to ask for a quiet room as this can make an enormous difference to how you feel the following morning.

HOW TO GET THERE AND BACK

Unless you have a friendly helicopter pilot on hand, it is impossible to

begin this journey at the source of the Loire, as it is perched on a 5000ft volcanic plug in the middle of the Massif Central. Instead, it is necessary to find a convenient and acceptable route to Le Gerbier de Jonc.

One option is to travel via the excellent European Bike Express, a coach and trailer run by the Cyclists' Touring Club in association with Bolero Travel, dedicated to taking cyclists and their bikes quickly and comfortably to a whole series of destinations across Europe. This will take you to Valence. From there it is possible to make the lung-searing ascent of the Massif Central via the D533 as far as St. Agrève (hotels), turning left onto the D120 to St. Martin de Valamas and then right onto the D237 to the source of the Loire, a distance of about 100km of almost non-stop ascent and descent with the emphasis on the former.

The climbing can be reduced by taking a second bus (which carries a maximum of two bikes) from the bus station in Valence as far as St. Agrève. This is the same route as that used to reach Le Puy for the commencement of the pilgrimage route to Santiago de Compostela. With that fact in mind, we decided to approach the Massif Central from further south via the Ardèche gorge. Although this is longer (just over 200km), it is far more spectacular and provides an added challenge. We therefore took the European Bike Express as far as the Roman city of Orange and the ride was started from there.

If the Valence/St. Agrève route is preferred or time is short, simply use this route to Le Gerbier de Jonc and begin the journey from Stage 6 in this guide.

There are a number of options for the return from St. Nazaire to the United Kingdom. One is to ride to St. Malo via Missillac, Redon, Montfort-sur-Meu and Dinan; another is to ride back as far as Savenay and take the train to St. Malo; and a third is to take the train directly from St. Nazaire to St. Malo. The latter, though very convenient if time is short, involves travelling by train back to Nantes before taking a connecting train north.

From St. Malo there are daily sailings to Portsmouth, but it may be necessary to book at least a day in advance in high season. This sea crossing is a long one (about 8 hours) and it is advisable to ensure that accommodation near to Portsmouth is available on arrival.

WHAT TO EXPECT ON THE JOURNEY

Roads

The majority of this journey is made on minor, well-surfaced roads with little or no traffic. There are a few short sections of cycle-way, which vary from smooth tarmac to rough track, although there is always an alternative to the latter. As far as possible, the route avoids major roads, although on the outskirts of some cities it is necessary to travel short stretches along them (many of these have cycle lanes painted on them but provide no protection from rampant motorists). I have a fear of roads with crash barriers – cyclists become the meat in a metal

Cycle lane through the centre of Nantes, Stage 22

sandwich – so the route attempts to avoid these like the plague, although new barriers are being erected all the time and there is no guarantee that this route is barrier-free.

Routes nationales (usually referred to as 'N roads' because their numbers are prefixed by the letter N) should, wherever possible, be avoided, as they are similar in nature to UK motorways. AutoRoutes are motorways and are prohibited to cyclists, as are all roads displaying a sign with a white car on a rectangular blue background.

Beware of the up-grading of roads. There are now quite a number of departmental roads (those preceded with the letter D) which are prohibited to cyclists (look for a blue square sign with a white car on it) because they have all the characteristics of full-blown motorways, including crash barriers. If you have doubts about a road, consult your IGN map to find a quiet alternative. They invariably exist.

Food and Drink

For those who have never cycled in France before, you are in for a gastro-nomic treat! Fresh food is abundant everywhere and there are plenty of cheap restaurants if you do not wish to prepare your own. Look for those which pro-vide meals for *ouvriers* ('workers').

From Orange to Le Puy, shops are few and far

between, and it is advisable to carry a day's food with you. After this, almost every village has some sort of store and markets, where food is at its freshest but not necessarily at its cheapest. Supermarkets, where food and drink are at their cheapest, are situated on the outskirts of most large towns.

Breakfast throughout France tends to be a light affair with crois-sants, jam, bread and coffee. Lunch, if taken in a restaurant, is usually a hearty meal, especially if it is taken where local workmen eat. Evening meals and those at Sunday lunchtime are legendary, although you will not be able to ride after them. Always look for places where locals eat and you cannot go wrong.

Water from the taps, unless it says *non-potable*, is perfectly safe to drink and most bartenders will fill your drinks bottle with ice-cold water at no charge. Beer is found everywhere but is not cheap except by the case in supermarkets. Wine, on the other hand, is much cheaper than in the

Market day in Orange

UK, but consuming large quantities halfway through the day does tend to curtail progress!

Language

The majority of the people you will meet on this journey will only speak French. They will not understand English even if you shout, so don't. Remember that a small amount of French goes a long way. You may need to ask the way, seek help, buy food (though no language is necessary at a supermarket) or find a bed for the night. Learn a few phrases and the sort of replies you may receive. It is no good asking a question if you cannot understand the answer. Learn the words for the parts of your bike and what might go wrong with them. If you can't remember them, write them down and carry a small dictionary.

If you cannot make yourself understood, ask if anyone speaks a little English. Most French are taught it at school but may be reluctant to try. If you are desperate, go to the nearest tourist office or bank. Someone there may be able to converse with you, if only in sign language.

Money

With the currency across mainland Europe being the Euro, there should be little difficulty in dealing with it. It is suggested that a small amount in Euros is carried from the UK, but it is far easier to withdraw money as you need it from the cash dispensers outside banks which are found in all

Old town square in Ruoms, Stage 4

small towns. (Make sure the dispenser displays the logo which is on your card.) The exchange rate is invariably better than the tourist rate, and when prompted you can choose to have the instructions for withdrawal displayed in English.

Small food outlets such as bakers and butchers expect to be paid in cash but many shops and supermarkets will accept credit cards. However, always check before you wheel your loaded trolley to the checkout. French cards have a chip set into them, not a magnetic strip as English cards do, and sometimes this needs to be explained to shop assistants or they may claim that your card is unacceptable.

Public telephones are to be found in every village and town. They are

19

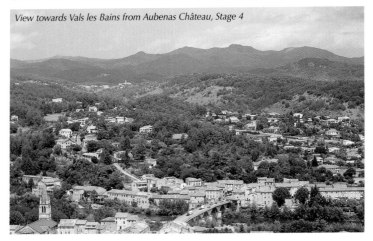

View towards Vals les Bains from Aubenas Château, Stage 4

invariably in full working order, but the majority only accept French phone cards. These are on sale at *tabacs* everywhere. A 50-unit card will cost just under £5, although cards with higher values are available and work out cheaper to use.

TOPOGRAPHY

The River Loire rises at one of the highest points in the Massif Central, a vast volcanic upland mass covering much of central southern France. On a clear day, the distant Alps can even be seen from here. The resilient rock formations have resulted in the infant Loire running through steep-sided gorges with strange and fascinating volcanic rock structures lining the banks. As a result it has been impossible for engineers to construct roads close to the river, and the route is forced to climb

and descend regularly whilst never straying far from the water's edge.

Along the first 500km of its length, the French have dammed the river at regular intervals to provide hydro-electric power, whilst at the same time creating long picturesque lakes. The riverside roads tend to run along the banks of these, providing magnificent views.

Once the River Loire has left the uplands of the Massif Central, it wanders indolently through an area which is really a part of the Paris Basin. Overlain with marls and clays, this is a perfect agricultural area. Pastureland stretches as far as the eye can see and the valley widens with little or no undulations. Vineyards, too, appear as the river flows north before it makes a violent swing to the west close to Orléans.

Here the underlying rock structure changes as the Loire cuts through limestone deposits, known as tufa, laid down on the bed of an ancient sea. The river becomes sandy with long islands, flooded in winter. The banks of the valley are quite steep, with troglodyte dwellings carved into the soft limestone.

Here is the garden of France, where fruit and vegetables of all kinds are grown in vast quantities. Vineyards are everywhere, producing some of the world's great wines. The sandy, fertile soil is heavily irrigated in the hot summer months before being inundated in winter and spring by floods when the snows melt on the Massif Central. The riding close to the river is easy and flat, but can become hilly any distance away from the river and even close to it on the Angevine Corniche.

Finally, the Loire nears the sea. The river is wide with many islands as it flows into its delta. Here is the Audubon Marais, an area of wetland with miles of narrow drainage ditches and streams forming a cobweb of water over this featureless landscape. The riding is easy now, but the scenery deteriorates as industry makes use of the banks of the Loire. Here are refineries, power stations and vast shipbuilding complexes that seem a million miles and as many years away from that tiny trickle of water flowing out of Le Gerbier de Jonc.

HOW TO USE THIS GUIDE

The whole journey from Orange to St. Nazaire has been divided into 23 riding stages of varying lengths, depending to some extent on the topography but more so on the places which should be visited en route and the time that may be spent exploring them. These divisions are purely arbitrary and need not be followed slavishly.

Leaving Orléans alongside the Loire on the cycleway, Stage 16

Chenin Blanc grapes grown for Anjou Blanc wine, Stage 20

The sketch maps in this guide are only meant to serve as a means of following the IGN maps easily. For convenience they are to be followed from bottom to top, so please check the orientation arrow on each map. They are not as accurate as the IGN maps nor are they as detailed, but they should give 'at a glance' indications of the route at road junctions, etc, and the names of villages and towns mentioned in the text.

Profiles of the first ten stages have been provided to give the cyclist an idea of the terrain during each stage. After Stage 10, the route is a gradual but steady descent, not worthy of a profile – downhill all the way! The occasional hill towards the end of the route is well documented and rarely, if ever, entails a climb or descent of more than 100m.

There are enough possible places to stay along the way that any stage can be lengthened or shortened according to the cyclist's whim. Of course, the Loire journey begins on Stage 6 of this book, and if an alternative route has been used to reach Le Gerbier de Jonc, then the guide should be used from that stage onwards.

Towns and villages which will be encountered along the way have been written in **bold** so that they can be used as a guide when route planning. Each significant township has a line to itself. The number of metres printed after it is its height above sea level and the numbers in brackets indicate the number of kilometres travelled from Orange/number of kilometres to St. Nazaire. For each town, the information given in *green italic* is a list of services, while that in brown is a guide to places of interest.

Wine tasting in Courthézon, Stage 1

STAGE 1

*Orange to Châteauneuf
du Pape (28km) – Total 28km*

Route	An easy ride to start the tour – one short climb before Châteauneuf du Pape
Surfaces	Good
See	Triumphal arch and Roman theatre in Orange (market day Thursday), vineyards around Courthézon, wine museum and ruined castle at Châteauneuf du Pape

This is an optional ride as a 'loosener' before the tour begins. If you wish to ignore this route, take the D17 out of Orange, cross the AutoRoute de Soleil and ride into Caderousse, picking up the Stage 2 route at this point.

Orange 28m (0/1371)
All facilities including information.
Orange is a city of sharp contrasts. It boasts two of the finest Roman buildings outside Rome, yet has one of the most comprehensive cycle-ways through a modern suburb in Provence. It contains a town centre full of shops, yet hosts one of the biggest street-markets in the region every Thursday morning. It has some of the friendliest people in France whilst being the home of the Front National party and its leader, Le Pen.

The Arc de Triomphe, standing rather forlornly in the middle of a roundabout, is covered in intricately carved

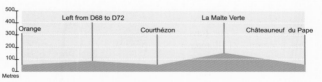

Stage 1 – Orange to Châteauneuf du Pape (28km)

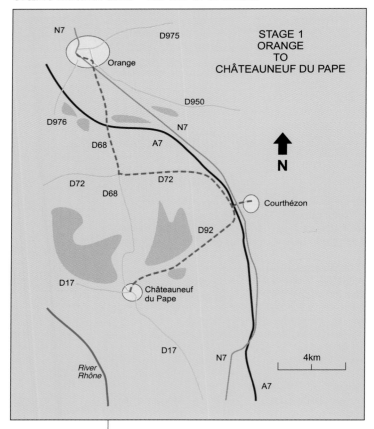

relief depicting Roman victories over Gaul. It is worth seeing, but great care needs to be taken when wheeling bikes across the very busy main road for a closer look.

No one should miss a visit to the Roman theatre, not that it is easy to miss. A colossal wall over 100m long and 36m high dominates the view. This is the back wall of the theatre pierced with archways which lead onto the stage area. Dominating everything is an enormous statue of the Emperor Augustus, standing in a niche high above the stage. The seating area, which is still capable of holding 10,000, rises in tiers, sheltered by the hill, St. Eutrope, from which a breathtaking view of the whole complex may be had.

It would be easy to spend a whole day in the city, especially if it is market day, when from six in the morning the streets are thronged with buyers and sellers alike. The air is filled with the sights, sounds and smells of Provence and the experience is, perhaps, the best introduction to this most glorious of cycle tours.

Leave Orange in a southerly direction on the D68. This does not look too promising as it passes through the city's older suburbs, but once the AutoRoute has been crossed the way is well signed. There are a number of unmarked minor roads to the left which should be ignored until a roundabout is reached with a road to the left, clearly signed to **Courthézon**.

Take this road, which heads in an easterly direction. It passes through numerous vineyards, for the Châteauneuf du Pape region, marked by a multitude of signs advertising individual domains, has now been reached. The ground here is covered with huge round pebbles, retaining the heat of the sun long into the night, thus hastening the ripening of the grapes. This road can be very exposed on windy days and, although it is quiet, care may need to be taken.

The road to Courthézon is good and obvious. At a minor crossroads go straight on, and at the next fork take the right-hand road, which is obviously the major route. As soon as the AutoRoute is reached, ride alongside it for a few metres before turning left and crossing it to reach the centre of the wine-producing town of

Courthézon 62m (16/1355)
Hotel, restaurant, bar, chambre d'hôte, bank, shops.
A sleepy town famous for its Châteauneuf du Pape and Côtes du Rhône wines, Courthézon embodies the spirit of north-western Provence. The main street is lined with

Arc de Triomphe in Orange

shady plane trees under which sit knots of old folk, whilst cicadas compete with the clack of boules as the dominant sound in this peaceful backwater. If time permits, visit one of the vineyards for a dégustation and explanation of the intricacies of wine production hereabouts.

Leave the town by re-crossing the AutoRoute and turn left before bearing right on the D92 towards **Châteauneuf du Pape**. This road is surprisingly hilly, with a number of steep, exposed climbs before it leads past numerous advertising hoardings into the centre of

Châteauneuf du Pape 100m (28/1343)
All facilities including information.
The historic town, famous world wide for its magnificent wines, has become the victim of its own popularity in the last few years. Almost every shop and cellar vies for customers with flags and signs, and the rural atmosphere still apparent in Courthézon has disappeared under a welter of commercialism. One has to climb up to the feudal castle to see the town, ringed by its vineyards, and realise how much it was dependent on its grapes in the past and how important tourism has become to its present and future economic prosperity.

Having said this, the wine is simply wonderful and should be tried even if it does break the bank. If possible, try to sample a Châteauneuf Blanc to experience one of the most complex wines in the world. The wine museum here is both extensive and informative and should be visited. A list of a good number of hotels and chambres d'hôtes is available from the tourist office in the centre of the town, although in mid-summer these become fully booked early in the day.

STAGE 2

Châteauneuf du Pape to
St. Martin d'Ardèche (54km) – Total 82km

Route	A longer but easy stretch of flat riding close to the Rhône
Surfaces	Good (busy round Pont St. Esprit)
See	Fortified town of Caderousse, Château Bosquet and Max Ernst mosaic in St. Martin d'Ardèche

Leave the town in a westerly direction on the D17. This skirts the far side of the ruined château and begins a long, steady descent, passing through seemingly endless vineyards towards the River Rhône.

At the T-junction with the D976, turn left onto it and almost immediately right under the AutoRoute onto the D237. This idyllic road winds besides backwaters of the Rhône until it reaches the quaint old town of

Caderousse 52m (38/1333)

Hotel, shops, campsite.
Having entered this fortified riverside town, it is well worth exploring it. There is a maze of narrow alleyways with a number of medieval buildings, including a fine clock tower in a good state of repair.

Leave the town, returning to the D237 and follow it for some way, ignoring minor junctions, before reaching a clearly signed junction with the D238. Turn left here

Stage 2 – Châteauneuf du Pape to St. Martin d'Ardèche (54km)

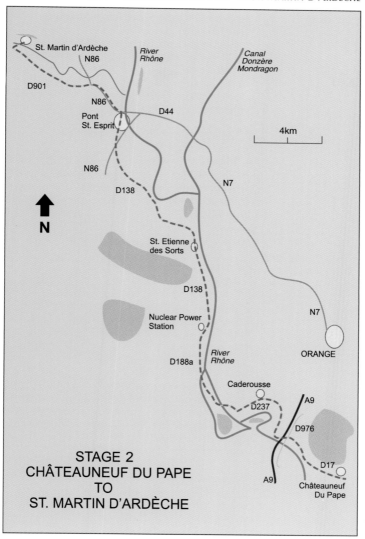

STAGE 2
CHÂTEAUNEUF DU PAPE
TO
ST. MARTIN D'ARDÈCHE

over a dam and bridge onto a long, narrow island in the River Rhône. The road now skirts the shore for a couple of kilometres before crossing a second bridge onto the D138a on the west bank of the Rhône. Ahead can be seen the nuclear power station at **Marcoule**. Head north, keeping the river close by on your right. Soon, thankfully, the power station is passed and left behind. The road becomes the D138 at this point before it heads into

St. Etienne des Sorts 32m (53/1318)
Bar (may be closed).
St. Etienne is a riverside village with an impressive church beside the Rhône. It appears that the village is being developed as a commuter town for Pont St. Esprit or the nearby nuclear power station.

Soon after leaving the village, the road drifts away from the river bank and swings north-west until it reaches

St. Georges 39m (56/1315)
No facilities.

Continue in a north-westerly direction along the D138 until a roundabout is reached on the outskirts of **Pont St. Esprit**. Cross the major road (D994) and climb up to the centre of the town.

Pont St. Esprit (64/1307)
All facilities including information.
Although this is a very busy town at a major crossing of the River Ardèche and in close proximity to the Rhône valley, it demands little of the sightseer's time. There is a large number of restaurants and bars which should easily satisfy any traveller's hunger and thirst.

Unfortunately, it is necessary to leave the town on the N86 in a north-westerly direction. This is an unpleasant, very busy road which is abandoned in 3km at a left turn onto the D908. This junction is obvious and well signed (follow the directions for the Ardèche gorge). The road is

*Max Ernst mosaic in
St. Martin d'Ardèche*

now much quieter, although there can still be a large
number of cars heading for the gorge in high season. The
route meanders through farmland and vineyards until it
reaches a T-junction with the D141.

Turn right here, and soon after passing a campsite an
iron bridge can be seen ahead crossing the River
Ardèche and leading into the centre of

St. Martin d'Ardèche 89m (82/1289)
*Information, hotels, chambres d'hôtes, restaurants, bars,
campsite, shops.*
Much of the town's popularity stems from its position
alongside the river. It is the terminus for canoeing trips
down the gorge and there is a large, sandy 'beach' opposite the town centre. Other places of interest include the
Romanesque church built on the site of a much earlier
chapel, the nearby Bosquet Château and many vineyards
offering the local brew. The surrealist artist Max Ernst
lived here, and there are usually exhibitions of his work
in the Office de Tourisme. An interesting mosaic to his
memory can be found in the town square.

STAGE 3

St. Martin d'Ardèche to
Les Mazes (44km) – Total 126km

Route	A hard stage with major climbs and some severe descents, easing after Vallon
Surfaces	Generally good, but tracks to viewing points are often unsuitable for bikes
See	Numerous views of Ardèche gorge, Pont d'Arc rock bridge, Vallon town hall
Warning	Inattentive drivers tend to wander while admiring views of gorge

This is a short stage, although there are times when it certainly does not feel like it! The gorge is climbed and descended a number of times – a stern test of legs and brakes. An added hazard is the number of cars whose drivers are busily looking at the view instead of the road ahead. These same motorists have a habit of overtaking and then braking or even reversing because they might have missed a viewpoint. They rarely seem to notice mere cyclists.

Leave St. Martin d'Ardèche on the D290 in a north-westerly direction. This road is more difficult to find than it first appears. If necessary, return to the iron bridge and follow the signs to the Ardèche gorge. The road now

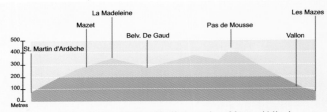

Stage 3 – St. Martin d'Ardèche to Les Mazes (44km)

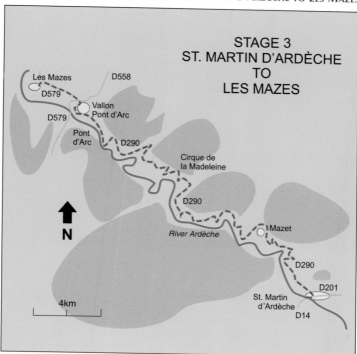

begins a long, steady ascent, with the river below to the left. The higher the road, the more spectacular the views become. Every so often, the route winds away from the river to negotiate a 'combe'. It is often at these points that height is lost and has to be regained.

Mazet 310m (90/1281)
Gîte d'étape.

The village can be seen and is signed to the left of the road, but there is no need to visit it. Instead, negotiate a couple of steep ascents and descents with numerous viewing points along the way. In this area, each limestone rock formation has been given a particular name or

The Ardèche gorge

attribute and is well signed. Many of the best viewpoints are away from the road and it is difficult to take laden bikes to them. Unless you have a stand, there are few places to lean bicycles here and this could cause a problem.

After an undulating section of road, a long ascent culminating in spectacular views ahead and below is followed by an extremely steep descent with sharp, awkward bends. Rims can become very hot here following continuous braking, and a pause to allow them to cool is advised. As the road levels out, a number of refreshment places herald the approach of the famous **Pont d'Arc** rock bridge over the Ardèche river. The riding is easy now, but the traffic can be extremely heavy. Watch out for a right turn which leads into Vallon. As soon as it has been taken, look for a road to the left which climbs steeply up to the town centre.

Vallon Pont d'Arc 150m (122/1249)
All facilities including information.
A bustling little town which has existed since prehistoric times, Vallon owes its prosperity to tourism in summer

and wine production throughout the year. This once for-tified town seems vastly overcrowded in summer, but it is worth visiting the town hall, which used to be the cas-tle. Inside are a number of beautiful Aubusson tapes-tries. The Office de Tourisme is very helpful, with a list of accommodation outside the town.

In order to find somewhere a little more peaceful to stay the night, leave the town via the D579 still heading north-west. After 4km, turn left into the village of

Les Mazes 89m (126/1245)
Campsite, chambres d'hôtes, restaurant, shop.
Although accommodation is limited, this tiny, quiet wine-growing village close to the river is infinitely more preferable to the noisy bustle of traffic in Vallon.

Vallon, Pont d'Arc, River Ardèche

STAGE 4
Les Mazes to Vals les Bains (44km) – Total 170km

Route	A hilly but pleasant ride with steep climbs and descents when visiting Balazuc and Aubenas
Surfaces	Good except in the village of Balazuc (dismount)
See	Medieval centre of Ruoms, whole of village of Balazuc, panorama from Château of Aubenas and Art Nouveau centre of Vals les Bains
Warning	There are dangerous tunnels between Aubenas and Labégude

This is an easy, relaxed ride prior to one of the toughest stages of the tour. Return to the D579 and turn left, heading towards Ruoms. The road climbs gently with good views of the surrounding hills, but it can be extremely busy as Ruoms is approached. The route at this point is lined with out-of-town hypermarkets and light industry served by many heavy lorries. In fact, the D579 no longer passes through Ruoms, but by-passes it, making it both difficult and dangerous to enter the town. The effort, however, is worthwhile.

Ruoms 130m (136/1235)
All facilities including information.
Ruoms is a pleasant country town with a very long history. The walled centre with its defensive towers maintains its

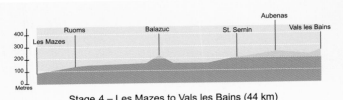

Stage 4 – Les Mazes to Vals les Bains (44 km)

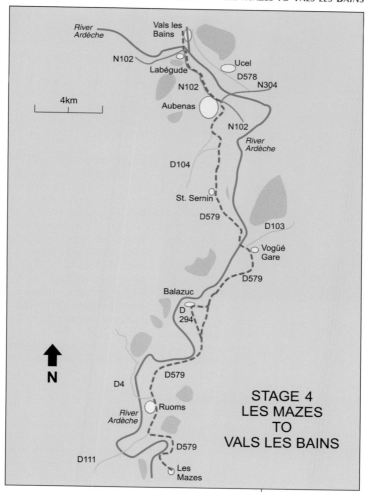

medieval atmosphere with a maze of narrow alleyways
and shady, quiet squares. The church dates back to the
12th century, and a priory was built here by the Brothers at

Medieval gateway into Ruoms

Cluny. The area immediately outside the ramparts maintained, at one time, a thriving silkworm-breeding industry, and traces of its existence can still be found, including a small museum devoted to it. Several profitable hours could easily be spent exploring here, especially if the market is in full swing.

Return once more to the D579, again taking the greatest care to regain the far carriageway and head north, always keeping the River Ardèche to your left.

The route now passes through a fruit-growing region, and road-side stalls selling luscious local produce can often be found. Having ridden through the village of **Pradons** with its campsite, gîte and shop, the road climbs steadily before a narrow road to the left, signed **Balazuc**, is encountered. Take this road as it rises steeply before attaining a col with terrific views in all directions and then descend equally steeply into the village centre.

Balazuc 207m (144/1227)

Restaurant, bar.

In high season this beautiful fortified medieval village, designated 'one of the most beautiful in France', and therefore one of the busiest, can become overrun with tourists. Many of the alleyways are cobbled and very steep, making it difficult to wheel cycles about. However, the church and its accompanying buildings and ramparts are fascinating, and time should be spent exploring the whole village and immersing oneself in its atmosphere. At the time of maximum silkworm and wine production in the 19th century, Balazuc had a population of almost 1000, but after a virus wiped out the silk-worms and phylloxera killed the vines, the population dropped to only just over 100 and has remained so up to the present day.

Return to the D579 and turn left towards Aubenas. The riding is relatively easy now and soon the road runs through

Vogüé Gare 165m (150/1221)
Shop and château.

Bear left with the main road, the D579, which soon crosses the river and runs round the outskirts of the village of **St. Sernin**, a quiet old community now that the road by-passes it. The village and its church are, nevertheless, worth visiting.

Aubenas: twinned with everybody!

On reaching the D104, turn right onto it. This is a noisy, bustling approach to **Aubenas**. The newly built road leads, via a series of roundabouts and crash barrier-lined dual carriageways, to the town of

Aubenas 200m (158/1213)
*All facilities
including information.*
A large, busy crossroads-town built on a steep bluff of land, Aubenas's main square and 12th-century château topped with a highly decorated roof quite naturally sit at the highest point, with the ancient quarter of the town ranged around them. Close by stands the Dôme Saint Benoît and the 13th-century church of St. Laurent. A magnificent view

Art Nouveau wall painting in Vals les Bains

towards the Auvergne and the mountains of the Massif Central can be had from here.

A decision must be made before climbing to this point as to whether the effort expended to attain this view is worthwhile. It is possible to ride on a lower road round the outskirts of Aubenas to cross the Ardèche river at the **Pont d'Aubenas** on the N304 and then turn immediately left onto the D578b through **Ucel** and into **Vals les Bains**.

However, if the desire to see the area through which the next day's ride is to be made proves too much, climb to the entrance of the château for the panorama and follow the signs downhill to Vals les Bains. It should be noted that this route follows an extremely fast and busy main road through a series of unpleasant, unlit tunnels before emerging in **Labégude**. Here the main road swings to the left, but the cyclists' route is to the right over a bridge crossing the River Ardèche, clearly signed to

Vals les Bains 260m (170/1201)
All facilities including information.
This is a strange, yet fascinating spa town. There is an atmosphere, still, of faded *fin de siècle* grandeur about the place. The River Volane flows through the centre of the town with roads on either side of it. Both sides are lined with restaurants, bars and hotels, many decorated in the Art Nouveau style.

Close to the river is a linear park where families can be seen strolling in the evenings or at weekends. The spa, whose water is renowned for curing diabetes and stomach upsets, is to be found at the upper end of the town and is no longer as grand as it used to be. Apart from tourism, the chief industry of Vals seems to be the production and sale of bottled water.

STAGE 5

Vals les Bains to
Le Gerbier de Jonc (39km) – Total 209km

Route	The hardest stage of the whole tour – relentless climbing with no respite
Surfaces	Good
See	Magnificent scenery throughout the stage, village of Antraigues, summit of Le Gerbier de Jonc (on foot) and source of the Loire
Warning	The second half of this ride can be very exposed in severe weather – check local forecasts before setting out

Although the distance is none too great, this is, without doubt, one of the most strenuous stages of the tour. The whole journey is one steady, unrelenting climb, becoming steeper as the stage progresses. There are few shops or bars along the way and it is advisable to carry as much liquid as possible and replenish empty water bottles wherever the chance appears. Nevertheless, in fine weather, this ride must be the highlight of the tour.

Leave Vals les Bains in a northerly direction by crossing one of several bridges over the River Volane onto the D578 so that the river is to the left. The road is already climbing gently. In minutes the houses are left behind as this wild river valley is followed. Occasionally, water-bottling factories will be seen close to the road but soon these disappear as the gradient gradually steepens. The road crosses and re-crosses the Volane river several times before it reaches the hill-top village of

Antraigues sur Volane 678m (179/1192)
Shops, bars, restaurant.
The centre of this rather quaint village, sometimes called the St. Tropez of the Massif Central because of its leafy squares and pavement cafés, does not have to be visited. The road skirts to the left of it and the ride up to

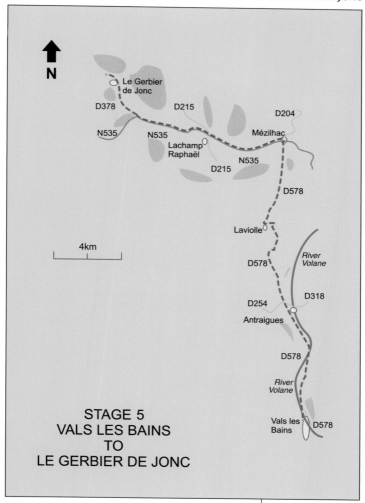

N

Le Gerbier
de Jonc

D378

D215

D204

N535

N535

Mézilhac

Lachamp
Raphaël

N535

D215

D578

Laviolle

4km

*River
Volane*

D578

D318

D254

Antraigues

D578

*River
Volane*

**STAGE 5
VALS LES BAINS
TO
LE GERBIER DE JONC**

Vals les
Bains

D578

the centre is quite steep, especially after the climb
which has already been made.

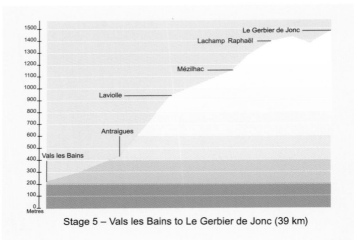

Stage 5 – Vals les Bains to Le Gerbier de Jonc (39 km)

Return and continue to climb on the D578, ignoring roads which cross the river and run at right angles to it. Instead cycle through breathtaking scenery until the small village of **Laviolle** appears ahead, high above the road. Although it seems impossible, the road will pass through this eyrie and from there onwards it will become noticeably steeper.

Eventually a road can be seen running along the horizon, high above. This road, when reached, passes through the centre of

Mézilhac 1149m (194/1177)
Hotels with restaurant and bars.
Positioned at a windswept col, a major road junction in the region, Mézilhac boasts two rather dreary hotels, one with life-size models of film stars outside, but little else.

This is a wild, desolate region even in mid-summer but the views over the volcano-dominated landscape demand lengthy perusal. This will also give time for aching muscles to recover a little!

Turn left onto the newly numbered N535 (shown on IGN maps as the D122) and continue climbing steeply towards

Strange visitors in Mézilhac

Lachamp Raphaël 1432m (199/1172)
No facilities.

Climb through the village along the same road before a sudden, short descent (the first of the stage). At the bottom of the hill turn right onto the D378, clearly signed to Le Gerbier de Jonc, and climb again heading towards a strange volcanic outcrop which looms over the hamlet of

Le Gerbier de Jonc 1551m (209/1162)
Information, hotel, restaurants, bars, gîte d'étape, gift shops.
What a strange place! The source of the River Loire is to be found, officially, at five separate springs dotted around the volcanic outcrop known as Le Gerbier de

Gîte d'étape below
Le Gerbier de Jonc

Jonc. The one most often visited is in a cow-shed close to the road which passes below this outcrop. It is visited by thousands of 'pilgrims' every year, and the road hereabouts is littered with souvenir stalls, craft shops and snack bars. There are even donkey rides! The *gîte d'étape* is excellent, and the key and nourishing meals can be had from the small restaurant next door.

STAGE 6

Le Gerbier de Jonc to
Goudet (54km) – Total 263km

Route	A very hilly ride with some breathtaking descents
Surfaces	Generally good – some tarmac break-up in places
See	Crater lake of Lac d'Issarlès, typical Auvergnat village of Issarlès and ruined castle at Goudet
Warning	Allow brakes to cool on long descents

Do not continue on the road past the souvenir stalls but
return to the point at which most of them begin (where
most cars are parked). From there the D116 begins a
thrilling descent. Within a few minutes you are treated
to your first sight of the infant Loire as it cascades down
the mountainside. Do not take the first road to the left

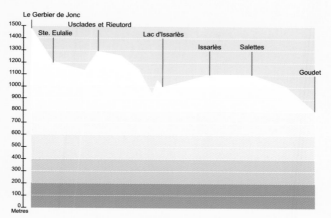

Stage 6 – Le Gerbier de Jonc to Goudet (54km)

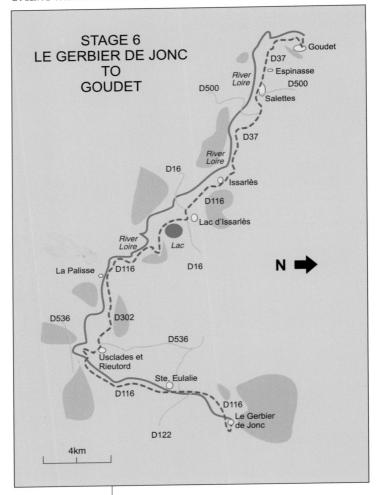

STAGE 6
LE GERBIER DE JONC
TO
GOUDET

(the D122) but fork left at the following junction, which may be unsigned and leads in 0.5km into the centre of the village of

**Ste. Eulalie 1199m
(214/1157)**
*Post office; hotel and bar
may be closed.*

Continue straight through
the village keeping close
to the river as the road
descends steadily through
the ever-widening Loire
valley. At a T-junction with
the D536, turn right, away
from the river, climbing
steeply towards trees. This
is a very long, arduous
climb, quite steep in
places, before the road
eventually twists and turns
into the hilltop village of

**Usclades et Rieutord
1298m (224/1147)**
*Gîte d'étape and bar,
both of which may be
closed in this isolated
community.*

*The infant Loire above
Ste. Eulalie*

Leave the village by turning left (west) opposite the
church on the D302. The road descends through magnificent scenery with a T-junction appearing ahead and
below. When this junction is reached, turn left onto the
D160 and follow it as far as the hamlet of **La Palisse** at a
bridge over the river. Before crossing the bridge, turn
right onto the D116, once more riding parallel to the
Loire, which is sometimes hidden from view by huge
piles of timber seasoning beside the road. The route
undulates regularly with tremendous panoramic views of
the Loire gorge from the highest points.

After a lengthy, steep descent, the road swings
sharply to the right and begins a muscle-searing ascent

to attain a col, beyond which a short, steep descent leads into the tourist haven of

Lac d'Issarlès 1004m (238/1133)

Hotels, bars, restaurants, shops.

The azure blue lake situated in the crater of an extinct volcano is where most people head for, but the old village, just to the left of the main road at the far end of the line of restaurants, is much more attractive.

Ride straight on out of the town until the D16 is reached. Turn left onto this wide, busy road, but in less than 1km swing right onto the D116 and follow this well-surfaced undulating road into the township of

Issarlès 1042m (244/1127)

Bar (could be closed).

This is a typical Auvergnat village with dark stone houses and a wide central square, through which the road runs.

At the far end of Issarlès, take the D116, left, signed to Le Monastier. In a short while this road becomes the D37. Stay on it until the road is joined from the left by the D500. Bear right onto it as it leads into the tiny farming hamlet of

Salettes 1165m (252/1119)

No facilities.

On the other side of the Loire, the fortress and village of Arlempdes may be glimpsed.

On the exit from Salettes, the D500 leaves to the right (signed to Le Monastier). Do **not** take this but follow the left turn into another farming village,

Espinasse 1084m (256/1115)

No facilities.

From here there is a very long, steep descent with fine views of **Goudet** Castle to the left. Finally, the road levels out in the picturesque riverside village of

Beaufort Castle in Goudet

Goudet 730m (263/1108)
Hotel, gîte d'étape, restaurants, bars, campsites.
An idyllic spot nestling beneath the mighty Beaufort Castle, cradled by the serpentine Loire, Goudet can be very busy in summer, but out of season it must rank as one of the most picturesque villages in France. The church with its multi-coloured pepper-pot roofs standing in a tiny square above the town should not be missed.

STAGE 7
Goudet to Le Puy en Velay (33km) – Total 296km

Route	A gentler stage than the previous two, although hilly as far as Solignac
Surfaces	Good except between Chadron and Solignac (gravel from quarries on road)
See	Church at St. Martin de Fugères, panorama of Loire gorge near Solignac, cathedral, Notre Dame de France, St. Michel d'Aiguille and medieval streets in Le Puy
Warning	Many heavy lorries leaving quarries around Solignac

This is a short, relatively easy stage. It allows time to be spent in Le Puy en Velay, if a whole day is not available to explore the town, although a week would be more appropriate.

Return to the edge of the village and take the D49 signed to **St. Martin de Fugères**. This is a very steep, 4km

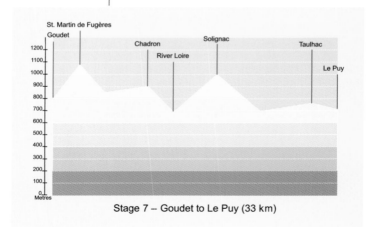

Stage 7 – Goudet to Le Puy (33 km)

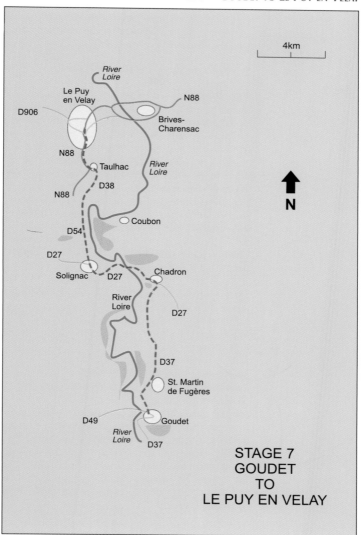

4km

River
Loire

Le Puy
en Velay

N88

D906

Brives-
Charensac

N88

Taulhac

D38

River
Loire

N88

N

Coubon

D54

D27

Solignac

D27

Chadron

River
Loire

D27

D37

St. Martin
de Fugères

D49

Goudet

River
Loire

D37

STAGE 7
GOUDET
TO
LE PUY EN VELAY

long climb which provides some of the finest volcanic scenery in Europe. More stops will be needed to admire the view than to retrieve lost energy!

St. Martin de Fugères 1120m (267/1104)
No facilities.
The village, with its ancient church dedicated to St. Martin, is worth exploring. It has tiny alleyways and a village square designed to protect its inhabitants from the wind. Towards the edges of the village there are panoramic views in all directions.

Leave to the left in a northerly direction on the D37. This is the beginning of a long, pleasant, slow descent. Continue straight ahead at the next two minor crossroads before a steady climb is encountered 1km before the village of

Chadron 850m (275/1096)
Bar and shop (may not be open).

There is no need to enter the village by turning right. Instead, turn left onto the D27 and descend through pastures and then woodland until the Loire is crossed at an iron bridge and a long, gentle climb is made into the busy village of

Solignac sur Loire 873m (279/1092)
Information in town hall, post office, hotel, campsite, restaurants, bars, shops.
Solignac stands atop a bluff overlooking the Loire gorge. In recent years it has been transformed from a simple medieval village, whose women-folk spent their days making lace, into a dormitory town for Le Puy. Nevertheless, the church, built on the remains of an earlier stronghold, should be visited. The circular fountain and water trough in the centre are typical of these Auvergnat villages.

Solignac, standing on a bluff above the Loire

Return to the entrance to the village and take a narrow road, the D54, which descends rapidly to the east of Solignac before levelling out parallel to the Loire. The road now undulates with a number of side roads leading to hamlets. Ignore them all until a T-junction with the D38 is reached.

Purists might decide to turn right via **Coubon** and ride round a huge loop of the Loire, but the most sensible way is to turn left here until the road meets the N88, bearing right as it does so. It is now only 1km of downhill riding to reach the centre of

Le Puy en Velay 640m (296/1075)
All facilities including information.
Le Puy, the capital of the Auvergne, demands time to be spent in it. Apart from having a large area to explore, it also houses some of the most fascinating, and at times breathtaking, monuments to be found anywhere in the world. It is built on top of an enormous extinct volcano with a number of gigantic volcanic plugs thrusting skywards, each with a different edifice built on top.

Perhaps the most incredible of these is the 13th-century church of St. Michel d'Aiguille, which looks as though some giant has taken it between his finger and thumb and dropped it exactly in place with not a single inch of land to spare. It always amazes people that there is a way up to visit it.

Staring down over her city stands the garishly painted Notre Dame de France, a gigantic statue of the Virgin and Child constructed from over 100 canons melted down after the Battle of Sebastopol. Once more, not only is it possible to climb up to this edifice, but the brave can even climb inside the statue to marvel at the panorama it provides from within its neck!

The colossal zebra-striped Cathedral of Le Puy dominates the town. Reached by either a lengthy series of steps or by winding, narrow medieval streets, it never ceases to amaze. Housed inside it is the famous Black Madonna of Le Puy, who keeps a watchful eye over the whole place, except at the feast of Assumption, when

The roofs of Le Puy from Notre Dame de France

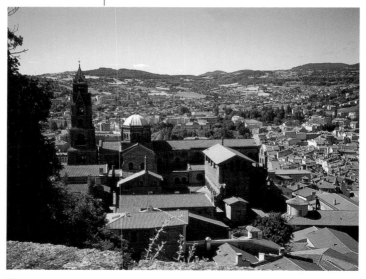

...pistachio nuts. Peas are a good source, too, so keep some in your freezer. They're handy when you're making a quick supper.

...potassium, which is ...the balance of fluid ...of potassium can le...

Leek & pea soup

Cook some peeled, sliced **potatoes** with washed and trimmed sliced **leeks** in a little butter for 10 minutes.

◆ Pour in hot **vegetable stock** to come 2cm above them, add a handful of **frozen peas** and simmer for 15 minutes.

◆ Remove from heat and add a handful of chopped **mint**. Liquidise until smooth. Serve with crème fraîche and chives.

Banana smooth...

Mash up a couple of **ban...** in a bowl. Add a good spic... with a handheld blender un... tablespoons of fat-free **natu...** of **honey**. ◆ Stir to combine, a... if you like it thinner. Serve in a t...

TOP TIPS

Fruit and vegetables are often a good sou... Most of this is found in the skin – so try to leave th... making sure that you wash the fruit and vegetab...

is one of the best sources of antioxidants betaine and anthocyanins, which destroy damaging free radicals.

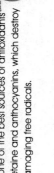

Granola & blueberry pot

Preheat the oven to 180C/350 Fan/Gas 6. Place some **mixed nuts and seeds** in a freezer bag, then bash with a rolling pin to crush ◆ Place in a bowl and add some **jumbo oats, raisins** and **runny honey.** ◆ Stir to mix together, then spread on a baking tray and bake for 20 minutes. Leave to cool and serve with **blueberries** and **natural yogurt.**

...ut in a large bowl with ...tuce leaves. ◆ Make a ...and one part **white wine** ...r and mustard. ◆ Toss with ...ped fresh **parsley** to serve.

steam or poach Fruit and veg can lose nutrients ...ooked, so eat them raw or steam or poach if you can. ...he fresher the food, the more vital nutrients it keeps. ◆

she is taken out to make sure her city and its citizens are still in order.

Le Puy is most famous, perhaps, for being the most important gathering point for the pilgrimage to Santiago de Compostela. Bishop Gottschalk of Le Puy was said to be the first to make the pilgrimage, and since then literally millions have followed in his footsteps. The old streets are lined with ancient pilgrim hospitals and hostels, and there are convents and monasteries dedicated to helping modern pilgrims who still leave for northern Spain every day of the year.

The home of lace making, Le Puy has many shops and galleries demonstrating and selling this fine art. There is still a lace school here, and visits to it can be arranged for a small fee. The Crozatier Museum, to be found in Le Puy's Edwardian park, contains many fine examples of this art as well as providing a museum of local history.

Give this extraordinary city time and it will reward you with several fascinating days filled with Auvergnat magic.

STAGE 8
Le Puy en Velay to
Le Pertuiset (79km) – Total 375km

Route	A long but relatively easy stage with one sharp climb through Retournac
Surfaces	Good throughout, although busy leaving Le Puy
See	Castle of Lavoûte, church at Chamalières, medieval village of Beauzac

As is often the case when leaving large cities, the exit from Le Puy is not easy to find. Ride in an easterly direction, then northerly along the D103. This is a multi-lane road with a number of junctions and can be very busy. If necessary, dismount and wheel your bike when attempting to cross the busiest intersections. If in doubt, follow the signs for Vorey and Retournac. From **Chadrac** onwards, the traffic melts away and the road, closely accompanied by the railway line, follows the bottom of the Loire gorge. After the hectic bustle of Le Puy, this is a peaceful, easy ride with excellent views along the Loire valley.

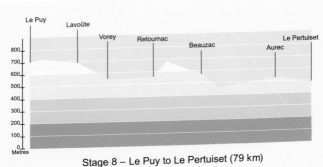

Stage 8 – Le Puy to Le Pertuiset (79 km)

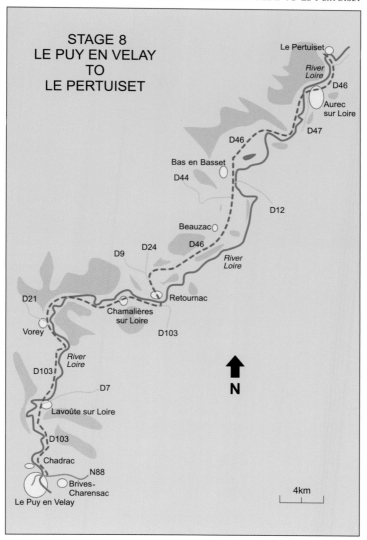

STAGE 8
LE PUY EN VELAY
TO
LE PERTUISET

Le Pertuiset

River Loire

D46

Aurec sur Loire

D47

D46

Bas en Basset

D44

D12

Beauzac

D24

D46

D9

River Loire

Retournac

Chamalières sur Loire

D21

D103

Vorey

River Loire

D103

D7

Lavoûte sur Loire

D103

Chadrac

N88

Brives-Charensac

Le Puy en Velay

N

4km

The Loire gorge near Chadrac

Follow the D103 until an enormous château looms to the left. This is the Polignac Lavoûte Château and marks the entrance to the village which is named after it.

Lavoûte sur Loire 557m (306/1065)
Shops, bars.
This small village has obviously grown here to service the 1000-year-old Polignac château of Lavoûte, which dominates everything from its position in a loop of the Loire. The village can be very busy with coach parties in high season, but the château, which contains letters from Marie Antoinette, is worth stopping to see, as is the beautiful little Romanesque church.

Staying on the D103, cross the river and enjoy a stretch of flat, easy riding mainly through arable farmland until the road leads into the busy little market and holiday town of

Vorey 538m (315/1056)
All facilities including information.

Vorey, a small tourist town, is situated at the confluence of the Arzon and Loire rivers and is renowned for its mild climate, bringing many water sports enthusiasts to the area. Nearby is the ruined château of Roche en Régnier.

Having ridden out of Vorey, the nature of the journey begins to change. The road leaves the valley floor at times and, therefore, becomes much more hilly. The valley now lives up to its title of the Loire gorge, with forested sides and stunning views. After crossing the railway, the road crosses the river as well and runs along the south bank for a number of kilometres until it enters the picturesque village of

Chamalières sur Loire 518m (323/1048)
Information but no facilities.
The ancient church and château stand guard over the river in this flower-bedecked village. It would be easy to sit all day in the remains of an early Benedictine cloister outside the remarkable church and watch the river glide by.

The Polignac Lavoûte Château in Lavoûte

However, it is not much further to a place where the scenery changes yet again. Stay on the south side of the Loire, and at the T-junction before the bridge turn left onto the D9 and cross it before a long, tedious climb through

Retournac 602m (328/1043)
All facilities including information.
Built on one of the flanks of the Loire gorge, the busy town straggles alongside the road which climbs high above the river. Apart from it being an ideal refreshment stop, there is little else to keep the cyclist here and there is still far to go.

At a junction which is reached high above Retournac, bear right onto the D46. This is not clearly signed but the route is obviously the major one (if in any doubt, do **not** take left-hand turns). Having reached the summit of this lengthy climb, enjoy a fast, steep descent into the medieval village of

Beauzac 647m (338/1033)
Information, hotels, restaurants, campsites, shops, bar.
Dismount to avoid cobbles round the village square, but do not miss this little gem of a village built of pale gold stone with its medieval church and crypt and narrow lanes.

The descent continues, although less steeply. The road has now changed its number to the D42, and after another 4km there is an awkward road junction. Take the left fork here, signed **Bas en Basset**, which was once a thriving river port. This is the D46 and virtually by-passes the town, which need not be entered. For a while now the road is flat, crossing what appears to be an old lake bed before once more entering the Loire gorge. The road climbs again, reaching high above the northern bank of the Loire before descending to cross a bridge into

Aurec sur Loire 565m (360/1011)
All facilities including information.
The town is situated along the eastern bank of the Loire where the valley widens somewhat. It is the hub of roads serving the surrounding area and is consequently very busy, with a series of difficult roundabouts. Being quite close to St. Étienne, it is becoming a dormitory town for that conurbation with attendant hypermarkets and shopping precinct.

A hydro-electric scheme on the Loire at this point has also increased traffic in the area. In reality, what was once a pleasant riverside town has become a place for cyclists to avoid. Its one claim to fame is in the manufacture of swords both for ceremonial and sporting events. Although there is a tourist office here, accommodation is scarce and expensive, and it is advisable to ride beyond Aurec before seeking out an overnight stay.

Stay on the D46 as far as the village of **Cornillon**, where the river is wider. This is a popular sailing and windsurfing centre, and accommodation may be available, particularly on a minor road which runs between the D46 and the river. However, if the D46 is followed as far as the Loire Bridge at **Le Pertuiset**, there is a choice of accommodation available.

At the entrance to the bridge, do not cross it but ride through a narrow tunnel to the right into a road lined with small hotels and restaurants. ▶ This is all that appears to exist in

Le Pertuiset 546m (375/996)
Hotels, restaurants, bars.

Note In July 2008 all the hotels in Le Pertuiset were closed for renovation.

STAGE 9
Le Pertuiset to Neulise (77km) – Total 452km

Route	The last long hill of the whole tour starts the stage – after that there is a steady descent with a sharp climb to finish it
Surfaces	Good
See	Panorama from Chambles, medieval centre of St. Just–St. Rambert, Loire gorge between Balbigny and Pinay
Warning	Very heavy traffic can be encountered in Balbigny – limited accommodation available after Balbigny

Leave Le Pertuiset by crossing the bridge and turning immediately right onto the D108. There now follows an 8km climb of a steady, rather than dramatic, nature. However, the views down into the Loire gorge certainly are dramatic as the road winds its way up to the 660m col at

Chambles 660m (382/989)
Hotel, bar, gîte d'étape and shop.
A windswept medieval village, clustered round its fortified 14th-century church and 18m-high siege tower built three centuries before that, seems to huddle against the

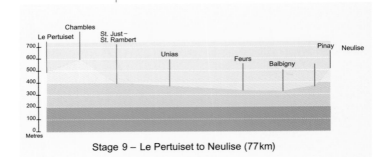

Stage 9 – Le Pertuiset to Neulise (77km)

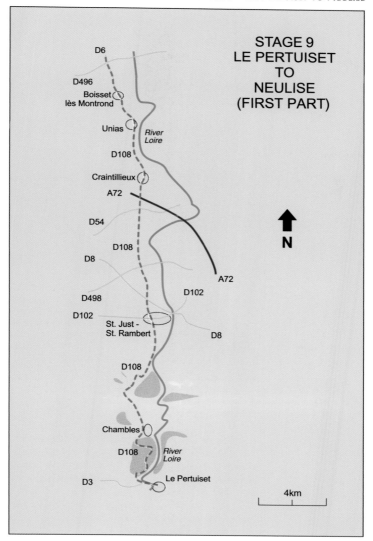

STAGE 9
LE PERTUISET
TO
NEULISE
(FIRST PART)

D6

D496

Boisset
lès Montrond

Unias

*River
Loire*

D108

Craintillieux

A72

D54

D108

D8

A72

D498

D102

D102

St. Just -
St. Rambert

D8

D108

Chambles

D108

*River
Loire*

D3

Le Pertuiset

N

4km

Eleventh-century siege tower in Chambles

icy blasts in this isolated spot. The views in all directions from here are truly spectacular.

Continue on the D108 as it begins its long descent into the Loire valley bottom. The whole atmosphere begins to change and soften as altitude is lost. Bungalows appear alongside the route and soon the road sweeps down into the centre of

St. Just–St. Rambert 382m (391/980)
All facilities including information.

There is no need to visit the river in this country market town, whose origins stretch back to the seventh century, as the route does not cross it. Instead ride into the pedestrianised centre and spend some time in its ancient quarter, visiting the church after which the town is named. It is a fine Romanesque building with beautifully carved capitals and sculpture. A visit to the Maison du Forez will provide a full, illustrated history to the town.

Ride out of St. Just–St. Rambert in a northerly direction on the D108 through a landscape considerably different from that encountered during the past week. Level farmland grazed by mahogany-coloured cattle stretches in all directions, with occasional fields of maize. Small hamlets, too small even to be called villages, appear at minor crossroads. The river begins to meander here, sometimes drifting several kilometres from the road, which follows an arrow-straight trajectory towards the village of

Craintilleux 352m (401/970)
No facilities.

*Loire gorge from
Chambles siege tower*

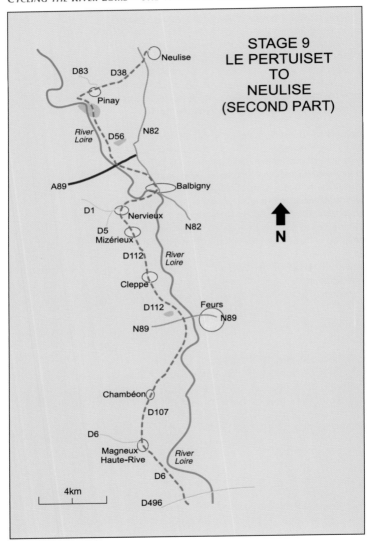

STAGE 9
LE PERTUISET
TO
NEULISE
(SECOND PART)

N

Continue riding along the D108 until the road follows the river more closely as it passes through

Unias 350m (405/966)
No facilities.

The route heads due north again through seemingly endless farmland until it arrives in the slightly larger village of

Boisset lès Montrond 336m (408/963)
Bar and restaurant.

There is little or no change in the scenery as the D108 crosses the N89 at a roundabout and heads for the village of **Magneux Haute-Rive**, where it changes its number to the D107 and heads for **Chambéon**.

Keeping to the right of this village, the road regains the banks of the Loire shortly before reaching the D89 at a T-junction. A right turn would lead over a bridge and into the town of **Feurs**. However, this is unnecessary unless provisions are needed. Instead take a left turn followed immediately by a right onto the D112 which leads into

Cleppe 346m (431/940)
No facilities.

After the excitement of the mountains and the Loire gorge, this section of the ride seems rather tedious, though perfectly pleasant. One wonders if the people who named the local villages felt the same in **Mizérieux** and **Nervieux**, where it is necessary to turn right in the centre onto the D1 before a quick descent into

Balbigny 321m (438/933)
All facilities including information.
Balbigny is a grey, rather threatening town, with the congested N82 bisecting it. Pleasant flower decorations in the main square cannot disguise the noise and volume of traffic here.

Unfortunately, in the centre of the town it is necessary to turn left onto the N82 for a couple of kilometres before, thankfully, taking a left fork onto the D56, which soon regains the bank of the River Loire as it passes under the A89 AutoRoute. The sides of the river here are particularly attractive, with cattle grazing the water meadows.

For another 3km the road hugs the river bank, providing beautiful views, then it changes its number to the D38 and makes a hairpin turn away from the river, climbing as far as the village of

Pinay 420m (446/925)
Bar, shop.

Overnight accommodation is scarce in these parts, and in order to find any it is necessary to ride away from the river. ◄ The Loire valley route is therefore left at this point. Continue through the village on the D38, which climbs steeply over a ridge before descending (crossing the N82) and climbing into the centre of

Note A great chambre d'hôte has now opened in St. Jodard, a mile beyond Pinay, so you may not need to detour to Neulise for accommodation.

Neulise 575m (452/919)
All facilities including information and chambre d'hôte.
The town was once as busy as Balbigny, but has become a backwater since it was by-passed by the N82.

STAGE 10
Neulise to Marcigny (74km) – Total 526km

Route	A series of short, steep hills until Roanne is reached, then easy riding
Surfaces	Adequate, with tarmac break-up along Loire gorge and on approach to Marcigny
See	Château de la Roche in mid-river, the Loire gorge as far as Villerest, the Loire Barrage at Villerest, the market (Mondays) and ancient buildings in Marcigny
Warning	The centre of Roanne is difficult to negotiate – dismount and walk through the pedestrian precinct

Unfortunately, it is necessary to ride back along the previous day's journey as far as **Pinay** to regain the route. At the crossroads (well signed) in the middle of Pinay turn right, and after one extremely hilly kilometre enter the attractive old town square at

St. Jodard 440m (459/912)
Chambre d'hôte, shops.
This stone-built village, dominated by its church and leafy square, need not detain the cyclist long, but provisions are available here at a small supermarket. It should

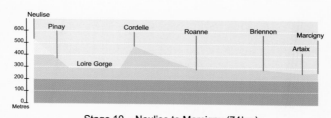

Stage 10 – Neulise to Marcigny (74km)

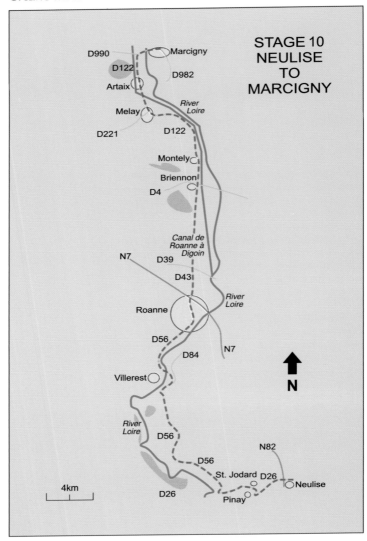

STAGE 10
NEULISE
TO
MARCIGNY

be noted that throughout the rest of the stage, apart from in the city of Roanne, accommodation is difficult to find, and the little that is available tends to be expensive by French standards.

Leave St. Jodard in a north-westerly direction heading towards the *gare* and **St. Paul de Vezelin**. Having passed the station, the road descends towards the Loire, but before crossing the bridge turn right onto the D56, which closely follows the eastern bank of the river. This is a spectacular ride with new vistas at every turn.

The first surprise is the **Château de la Roche**, a magnificent building sitting in the middle of the river like some fairy-tale castle. Its setting is well-nigh perfect. From here to the village of Villerest, the river widens and the valley deepens (with some help from the great barrage at Villerest) to form yet another Loire gorge. The D56 climbs and dives along the valley side before it turns away from the river at an awkward T-junction to the right. From here there is a long, steady climb to gain the top of a ridge, providing good views in all directions.

Gigantic sundial above Villerest

A strange monument close to a hotel on the left turns out to be a gigantic sundial. From here, the panoramas up and down the valley are superb.

Finally, the road makes a long, steep descent towards the barrage, which can be seen straddling the Loire far below. The road eventually crosses this, providing the spectacular sight of the river emerging through a relatively narrow pipe, providing a multi-coloured plume of spray which hangs in the air far down the valley. Who says hydro-electric schemes have to be ugly?

It appears from the map that the route takes the cyclist through the village of **Villerest**, but this is not the case. Having crossed the barrage, turn right, keeping as close to the river bank as possible until at a T-junction on a hill it is necessary to turn right towards the river and then left before crossing it, following signs for **Roanne**. This road looks unpromising at first, but it clings to the west bank of the river which will eventually flow through Roanne.

Soon housing appears on both sides of the road as the city suburbs are reached. Continue along this road until signs to the city centre are met. These should be followed into the heart of

Roanne 293m (485/886)
All facilities including information.
Roanne is a large, busy city, the centre of which is pedestrianised. Sadly, for its size, it has little to detain the cyclist save for a dungeon in the château, a Renaissance church and a fine arts and textile museum. It appears that someone forgot to put up road signs when they designed the centre of Roanne. The result is clear directions into the city centre but none out of it. Ask for the road to Briennon and the D43 should eventually be found.

Leave the city on the D43 in a northerly direction, passing beneath the N7, which appears to be an AutoRoute at this point. The route passes through modern suburbs with sports grounds before crossing the D39 into open countryside. The riding for the rest of the stage is easy. The road runs alongside the Roanne– Digoin Canal, which itself runs parallel to the gently meandering Loire.

Having passed through

Briennon 275m (502/869)
No facilities.

the road crosses the canal and then runs along its bank. This is an idyllic stretch of waterway, with hamlets huddled close to the banks and pleasure boats plying their trade.

Stay alongside the canal as it swings west away from the river, where the road number changes to the D122 before entering the village of

Melay 320m (511/860)
Gîte d'étape, which may only take pre-booked groups; bar, shops.

Pass through this village and continue following the D122 as far as a road to the left which leads, after a couple of hundred metres, into the ancient community of

Artaix 251m (519/852)
No facilities, but this tiny village which must, at one time, have thrived on canal trade, deserves exploration.

Return to the D122 and follow it as it flows between the river and the canal as far as

Chambilly 250m (519/852)
Hotel (may be closed).

Turn right and cross the river, and immediately afterwards negotiate an awkward road junction before riding up into the centre of

Marcigny 275m (526/845)
All facilities including information.

*Market day in
Marcigny*

A market town of great antiquity, Marcigny sits to the east of and slightly higher than the Loire valley upon whose trade it grew. The fine town square is thronged on market days, as it is the largest for some distance around. There is evidence of Romanesque architecture everywhere, whilst the majority of the buildings in the centre are early 19th century in origin. Although accommodation (hotels and chambres d'hôtes) is plentiful, it is unusually expensive.

STAGE 11

Marcigny to
Gannay sur Loire (82km) – Total 608km

Route	A long but pleasant ride following the flood plain of the Loire
Surfaces	Good throughout
See	Baugy church, the Canal de Roanne à Digoin, the Abbaye de Sept Fonts
Warning	Expect relentless heavy traffic on the approach to and in the centre of Digoin

Close attention to IGN map 43 will help to find the exit from Marcigny. This can be difficult because certain roads including the D982 have recently been re-aligned and widened, and are now unable to be used by cyclists, an increasing problem in France. Take the C3 north out of Marcigny, just after crossing the D982. This meanders through leafy suburbs before running along the edge of the flood plain of the Loire. The first small settlement (its name apparently a derivation of the word 'boggy') to be encountered is

Baugy 254m (529/842)
No facilities.
A sign should tempt you to visit the beautiful Romanesque church here (one of a series of 30 such churches and chapels in the area). It is certainly one of the oldest in the region, dating back to the 11th century. Look for the carvings of animal musicians.

This road becomes increasingly rural as it progresses north. Time does not appear to have had any effect on this area, where farmers still tend their fields by hand and cattle munch the long green grass of the water meadows.
    At the T-junction, turn left into

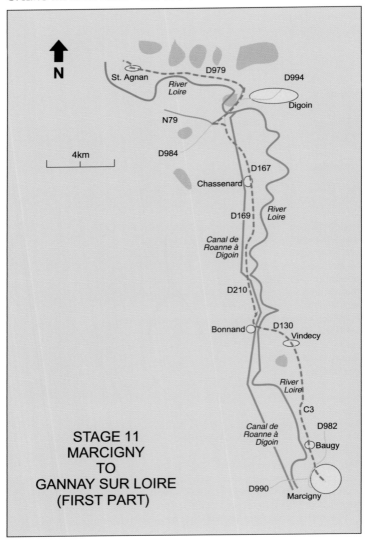

N

St. Agnan

D979

River
Loire

D994

Digoin

N79

D984

4km

D167

Chassenard

D169

River
Loire

Canal de
Roanne à
Digoin

D210

Bonnand

D130

Vindecy

River
Loire

C3

Canal de
Roanne à
Digoin

D982

Baugy

STAGE 11
MARCIGNY
TO
GANNAY SUR LOIRE
(FIRST PART)

D990

Marcigny

Vindecy 240m (535/836)
No facilities.

Now cross the River Loire and ride into

Bonnand 245m (538/833)
No facilities.

Turn right onto the D210 and continue this peaceful ride through undiscovered central France. The road is virtually flat as it runs alongside both the Loire and the Roanne à Digoin Canal. Occasional bridges over the waterways are the steepest inclines encountered. It must be borne in mind, however, that there are virtually no facilities available between Marcigny and Digoin.
    Having passed through

Chassenard 247m (547/824)
No facilities.

do **not** fork left on the D167 towards Molinet and St. Martin but keep ahead on the D169, taking a left/right dog-leg in 1km before riding straight ahead to join the N79. Turn right onto this road at the T-junction. This is an extremely busy and dangerous road, and cyclists may prefer to dismount, as the distance from the junction to the town centre is less than 1km and is lined with hypermarkets and the usual out-of-town shopping malls.

Digoin 234m (554/817)
All facilities including information.
The dangerous nature of the roads around Digoin might well persuade cyclists to follow the directions given here and avoid the town centre and its gridlock traffic problems.

Having crossed the River Loire, taking the utmost care (it is safer to dismount), turn left off the N79 onto the D979 at multiple traffic lights. This road is not as busy as the *route nationale*, but there is still a considerable amount of traffic

79

using it at all times of the day, and great care should be exercised.

The road is pleasant, however, with good views of the Loire meandering to the left below the road. The way is no longer flat, but hills are no more than gentle undulations and there are occasional flat stretches along the river bank.

St. Agnan 246m (563/808)
Bar and restaurants

provides a welcome lunch break on this long stage.

Having passed through the centre of

Gilly sur Loire 224 (575/796)
Bar and shop

look for a railway bridge crossing both the road and the Loire. Immediately after this take the roadbridge (the D480) to the left, which passes over the river, and ride the short distance into

Diou 220m (578/793)
Hotel, gîte d'étape, bar, shops.

This is the last refreshment stop for over 40km. Once more the busy and dangerous N79 must be negotiated as it passes through the village. Turn right onto it (you may wish to dismount), and at the end of the village fork right off it onto the quiet D15, which soon joins the bank of the Canal Latéral à la Loire. For the rest of the stage the road will never be far from this canal, whilst the River Loire meanders further away to the right.

Soon a large abbey appears ahead. This is the **Abbaye de Sept Fonts**. It is still in operation, and visits round it can be arranged. Opposite its entrance the D15 leads left to a T-junction, where it now turns right through quite remarkable scenery. Gone is the rural idyll – replaced by heavy engineering works. Enormous pipes litter the area, and iron foundries dominate the

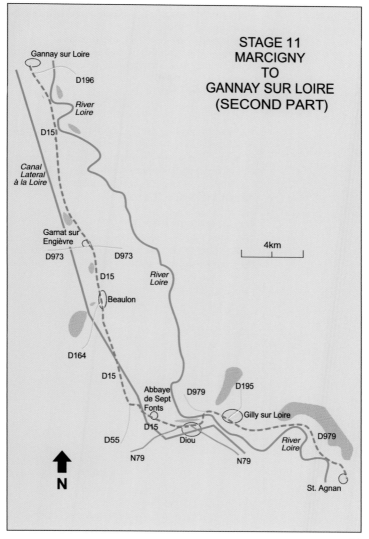

STAGE 11
MARCIGNY
TO
GANNAY SUR LOIRE
(SECOND PART)

Gannay sur Loire

D196

River Loire

D15

Canal Lateral à la Loire

4km

Garnat sur Engièvre

D973   D973

D15   *River Loire*

Beaulon

D164

D15

Abbaye de Sept Fonts   D979   D195

Gilly sur Loire

D15

D55   Diou   *River Loire*   D979

N79   N79

St. Agnan

N

skyline until, just as abruptly, they are replaced by fields full of browsing cattle. Industry will not be encountered again for the rest of the stage.

The way now runs in the bottom of the Loire flood plain and soon leads into the rural community of

Beaulon 214m (590/781)
No facilities.

The next stretch along the D15 can be rather daunting as no villages or even hamlets are ridden through for many kilometres. The scenery is pleasant enough, but there is little to divert the eye from the tarmac stretching ahead.

After such a long stretch in the saddle it is a relief to ride into the farming village of

Gannay sur Loire 201m (608/763)
Chambre d'hôte (the sign to this may be hidden in a hedge to the right of the road at the entrance to the village), bar, restaurant (may be closed).

STAGE 12

Gannay sur Loire to Nevers (57km) – Total 665km

Route	An easy if uninspiring run along the valley bottom closer to the canal than the river as far as Nevers
Surfaces	Good throughout
See	The canal-side villages of Avril sur Loire (church) and Fleury sur Loire, the medieval quarter of Nevers, the cathedral (stained glass) and the old château.

The ride takes little more than half a day, but it allows sufficient time to explore Nevers, in which it is worth spending time.

Leave Gannay in a north-westerly direction and continue riding along the D15 through the flood plain of the River Loire with the canal close at hand. The scenery takes over where it left off in the previous stage, with lush water meadows and scattered farmsteads.

Lamenay sur Loire 200m (613/758)
No facilities

is passed without noticing, but from here on the canal is alongside the road. Mahogany-coloured cattle graze, and the only traffic likely to be encountered is a farm tractor.

At the T-junction with the D978a, turn left towards **Decize**. This is a rather faceless township which hardly warrants a visit. Instead of riding into the town centre, turn left at the second roundabout and follow signs to

Avril sur Loire 220m (638/733)
No facilities.
This canal-side village should not be missed. A beautiful little Romanesque church boasts a truly eerie crypt with no indication as to its history. Added to this, some

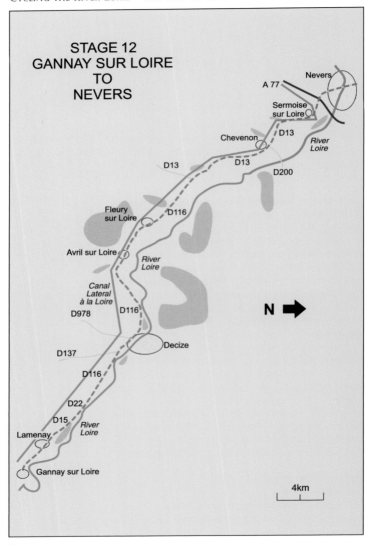

interesting carvings make this a place in which to spend some time.

Continue hugging the canal bank until the road runs into the centre of the little township of

Fleury sur Loire 192m (642/729)
Post office, shop.

A long stretch of riding along the D116, which soon changes its number to the D13, heading generally in a north-westerly direction, continues to follow the Loire and the canal. On approaching **Chevenon**, the road towards the town centre is to the right of a roundabout. As there is no need to visit this small town, continue on the D13, straight ahead.

For the first time in a couple of stages the road begins to climb steadily until **Sermoise sur Loire** should be glimpsed (but not visited) away to the left. The road now begins a long, steady descent. On reaching the AutoRoute, pass beneath it and follow the obvious signs over the Loire Bridge to enter

Nevers 202m (665/706)
All facilities including information.
Many of the streets are still cobbled in this pleasant ancient city – cyclists beware! The shopping area is tucked away from the city centre and encroaches on the ancient quarter to neither's detriment. Accommodation in Nevers itself is scarce and expensive, but a helpful tourist office should be able to find something, although they are reluctant to telephone on clients' behalf.

An interesting feature of the city is a blue line painted on roads and pavements, leading visitors to the most important monuments – an excellent and simple idea which really works.

Apart from the river, the main feature of the town is its cathedral, dedicated to St. Cyr–Ste. Julitte. It was severely damaged during the Second World War, but has been completely rebuilt with some of the most startling

Exterior view of Nevers Cathedral

stained-glass windows to be found in France. It also boasts the unusual distinction of having two choirs. Other ecclesiastical monuments worthy of a visit include the Abbey of Saint Martin buildings, the 11th-century St. Étienne church and that of St. Pierre.

The 19th-century town hall is one of a number of secular buildings which demands attention. These include the Ducal Palace, the theatre and the 17th-century Château de la Gloriette. A full exploration of all the above and many other interesting areas of the city would take at least a full day.

The magnificent stained glass inside Nevers Cathedral

STAGE 13
Nevers to Sancerre (67km) – Total 732km

Route	A ride with a sting in its tail! The roads tend to undulate towards the end of the stage with a steep climb to Sancerre
Surfaces	Good apart from the centre of Sancerre (cobbles and worse)
See	The priory and medieval centre of La Charité, the panorama from Sancerre with its ancient centre. Taste the wine!
Warning	The exit from Nevers is always busy and can be dangerous – keep to the riverside if possible

Leaving the city of Nevers can be both difficult and dangerous. The obvious route is to take the D40 in a westerly direction, but this road is now of motorway standard with its attendant hazards. It is also lined with out-of-town shopping malls served by enormous juggernauts and visited by large numbers of motorists. A quieter way is to travel in a south-westerly direction alongside the Loire on the D504 before taking a right turn onto the D266 into **Marzy**. Turn left in the village and then turn right onto the D131 for 5km. This will emerge at a T-junction with the D40 on the edge of **Fourchambault** (which need not be entered). Turn left here, crossing the bridge over the Loire leading into the hamlet of **Givry**. Here turn right onto the D12 and ride across the flood plain of the river before entering the village of

Cours les Barres 162m (683/688)
Bar.

Turn right onto the D920 at the entrance to the village and then fork right again onto the D45 at its exit. This pleasant canal-side road soon leads into

Marseille les Aubigny 162m (689/682)
Post office and bar.

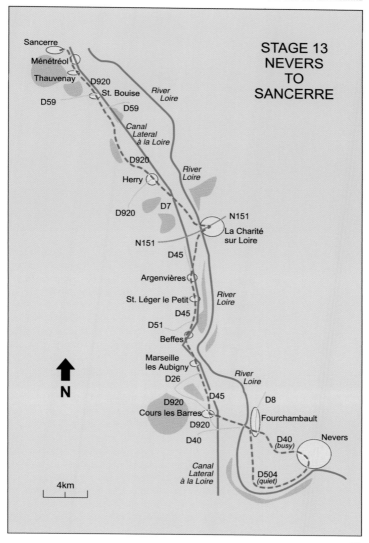

Sancerre
Ménétréol
Thauvenay
D59
D920
St. Bouise
D59
River Loire
Canal Lateral à la Loire
D920
River Loire
Herry
D920
D7
N151
La Charité sur Loire
N151
D45
Argenvières
St. Léger le Petit
River Loire
D45
D51
Beffes
Marseille les Aubigny
D26
River Loire
D920
D45
D8
Cours les Barres
D920
Fourchambault
D40
Nevers
D40 *(busy)*
D504 *(quiet)*
Canal Lateral à la Loire

STAGE 13
NEVERS
TO
SANCERRE

N

4km

Riverside industry between Nevers and La Charité

The road, whilst keeping to the canal bank, is lined with small-holdings and farmsteads until, having by-passed **Argenvières**, the route forks right on the D45E and heads for the river bank and the town on its opposite side, **La Charité sur Loire**.

When the N151 is reached, turn right to cross the fine bridge over the River Loire and ride up to the centre of the ancient pilgrimage town of

La Charité sur Loire 162m (703/668)
All facilities including information.
The priory dominates everything in this medieval town. It and its related buildings must, at one time, have covered much of the area. Now little remains except the church which is, nevertheless, very impressive and some ecclesiastical buildings. Narrow medieval streets wind up from the river bank and some time can be spent admiring both the secular and religious architecture.

The main priory church dates back to the 11th century, and its tower to the 12th. It was often known as the 'elder daughter' church to the great abbey at Cluny, which was, in the 12th century, the greatest church in

Christendom. Around and close to the priory are the monastic buildings in various states of repair, but there is still no doubt about the religious importance of this place. It is, today, a UNESCO World Heritage Site.

Tympanum of the priory in La Charité sur Loire

To leave La Charité, re-cross the bridge on the N151 and take an immediate right turn onto the D7. For a couple of kilometres this road runs along the river bank before swinging away to the left as it crosses the flood plain of the Loire towards a line of low hills to the left. The surface is excellent and the pleasant farm scenery encountered earlier continues.

Herry 180m (711/660)
Bar.

This village marks a change in riding conditions and a change of road number (to the D920). For the first time in several days the road begins to undulate. The horizons widen and a lack of trees makes it feel more exposed. On reaching

St. Bouise 200m (722/649)
No facilities

it is noticeable that the road begins to climb and much higher hills can be seen rising to the west. The climb continues through **Thauvenay**, and, having reached **Ménétréol sous Sancerre**, the route begins a steep, lengthy ascent among Sancerre vineyards by way of a series of hairpin bends until it emerges, eventually, in the famous hill-top township of

Sancerre 356m (732/639)
All facilities including information.
A lovely, lofty old town which tourism does not seem to have spoilt. The wine, of course, on which Sancerre has built its reputation, is to be found on sale everywhere, but the Sancerrois seem to have kept a sense of proportion. The town square is, as might be expected, lined with restaurants, but few trinket shops are to be found. Wine growing is a serious business, and the ephemera of the tourist industry has not been allowed to interfere with it.

The town should not be left without a visit to the church of Notre Dame de Sancerre, which took almost 100 years to build, and to the belfry, whose chequered history lives on even today.

The vineyards which surround the town cover 2350 hectares and produce 140,000 hectolitres per year, the grapes being of the Sauvignon and Pinot Noir varieties. The white, woody-flavoured Sancerre has been awarded AOC status since 1936, but the reds and rosés with their aromas of cherries did not achieve it until 1959.

STAGE 14

Sancerre to Briare le Canal (50km) – Total 782km

Route	A long descent followed by a pleasant, easy ride beside the Loire and canal
Surfaces	Good apart from the crossing of the Pont Canal into Briare
See	The church in St. Satur, the bustling market town of Cosne and Briare with its complex canal system and its Mosaic and Enamel Museum

Leave Sancerre in a northerly direction on the D955 following signs for **St. Satur**. The descent is steep and care needs to be taken, as the road can be very busy. In the centre of St. Satur, with its huge 14th-century abbey church alongside the road, take a left turn, north, on the D955.

This is an excellent, fairly quiet road which runs on the west bank of the Canal Latéral à la Loire, a canal which is often crowded with both pleasure craft and working barges. After about 10km, keeping to the D955, turn right at a T-junction and ride over two impressive bridges to enter the town of

Cosne Cours sur Loire 184m (747/624)
All facilities including information.
The centre of this bustling, flower-bedecked town is very attractive, with old buildings alongside modern facilities. The church of Saint Agnan is a 12th-century edifice built on a much earlier site. Nearby is the Forges de la Chaussade, where anchors were manufactured for the navy.

This is the centre of a major wine production area, the Coteaux du Giennois, which dates back to the second century AD. It is the last sizeable town encountered before the end of the stage, and is ideal for replenishing supplies.

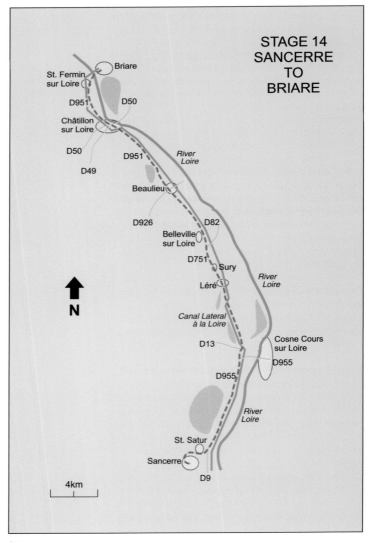

STAGE 14
SANCERRE
TO
BRIARE

Briare
St. Fermin
sur Loire
D951
D50
Châtillon
sur Loire
D50
D951
D49
River
Loire
Beaulieu
D926
D82
Belleville
sur Loire
D751
Sury
Léré
River
Loire
Canal Lateral
à la Loire
Cosne Cours
sur Loire
D13
D955
D955
River
Loire
St. Satur
Sancerre
D9
N
4km

To leave Cosne, re-cross the two bridges and turn right onto the D751, signed to **Léré**, keeping to that road (to the right) at the fork after another 1km. Unfortunately, this is a quite busy, not very interesting road through suburban villages. The route wanders up to 2km away from the river, but is never more than a few metres from the canal.

Léré 143m (757/614)
No facilities except campsite.
The collegiate church dedicated to St. Martin has a Romanesque nave but a ninth-century crypt.

Léré is one of a series of similar villages with little to detain the cyclist. Basic 20th-century architecture predominates and facilities of any sort are at a premium. (**Note:** The gîte d'étape at **Sury** no longer seems to be operating.)
　　Continue on the D751 as it passes through

Belleville sur Loire 140m (762/609)
No facilities.

The road now begins to undulate gently before dropping into the village of

Beaulieu 160m (767/604)
Post office.

The undulations become more pronounced as the road, now the D951, leaves Beaulieu in a northerly direction. It also leaves the banks of the canal, which stays in the flood plain of the Loire. The scenery hereabouts becomes more interesting, with ancient hamlets and woodland appearing. Finally the road drops back down into the flood plain as it enters the small town of

Châtillon sur Loire 135m (775/596)
All facilities including information and supermarket.

The D951 now runs between the river and the canal, with bridges and embankments appearing. This is a fascinating

The banks of the Loire at Briare

stretch of the route, with traces of industrial archaeology to be found everywhere.

Having passed through the village of **St. Fermin sur Loire**, look out for a rough track which climbs steeply to the right, leaving the D951 and signed 'Pont Canal'. This does not look very inviting, but it quickly leads to the canal bank. Here begins the longest (662m) canal aqueduct in Europe, which took five years to build. It has a wide cycle/footway on both sides and it should be followed as it crosses the valley of the River Loire before leading into the outskirts of

Briare le Canal 150m (782/589)
All facilities including information.

Briare should be explored thoroughly, as it has a surprise round almost every corner. It is one of the canal centres of France, and its many basins with connecting bridges are lined with flowers. Pleasure boats offer lazy trips along the canals, and the evening can be spent at canalside restaurants or bars.

Briare Church is decorated with Bapterosses' mosaics

Bapterosses Enamel sign in Briare

Briare's other great claim to fame is its mosaic industry. A fascinating museum housed in part of the Bapterosses Mosaic and Enamel Works traces how this small town produced literally billions of tiles and glass beads, the latter to fulfil the inexhaustible appetite of African countries. The industry is still in operation, and on closer inspection it will become apparent that most of the town's buildings, including the huge church, are decorated with tiles and mosaics.

STAGE 15

Briare le Canal to
St. Benoît sur Loire (51km) – Total 833km

Route	An enjoyable, flat ride through the first signs of the Garden of France
Surfaces	Good after Briare is left
See	Restored Gien, the Château of Sully sur Loire and the magnificent abbey of St. Benoît sur Loire
Warning	Do not take the Loire Cycleway on this stage – see below for exit to Briare

Do **not** attempt to leave Briare on the D952 to the north of the River Loire. Although it is signed for cyclists, with a marked cycle-way for the first couple of kilometres, this crash-barrier-lined road into Gien is as busy and dangerous as any motorway and should be avoided at all costs. Instead, return over the Pont Canal and turn right onto the D951.

Now the scenery changes subtly. The route has entered the Garden of France. The road is lined with fruit trees, fields of asparagus, vegetables and cereals, some of which can be purchased at the roadside. For the first time in days there is no canal to follow. The River Loire, however, is still close at hand and the road runs along its south western bank into

Gien 130m (795/576)
All facilities including information.
There is no need to ride into the centre of Gien, which is famous for its high-glaze ceramics, unless you wish to visit its château and church close to the quay. Much of the town was destroyed during the Second World War, but it has been tastefully restored. The best view of the town is from the tree-lined D951 by which you approach it.

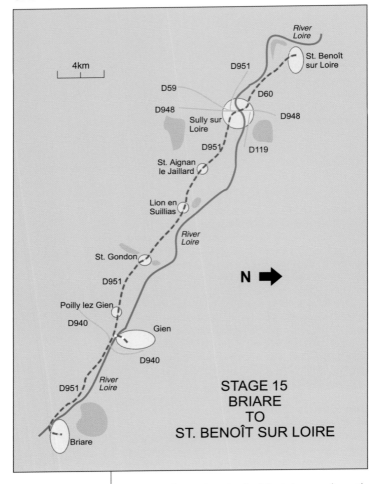

River
Loire

D951

St. Benoît
sur Loire

D59

D60

D948

D948

Sully sur
Loire

D951

D119

St. Aignan
le Jaillard

Lion en
Suillias

River
Loire

St. Gondon

N ➡

D951

Poilly lez Gien

D940

Gien

D940

D951

River
Loire

STAGE 15
BRIARE
TO
ST. BENOÎT SUR LOIRE

Briare

4km

Staying on the southern bank of the Loire, pass beneath
the D940 and, instead of crossing the bridge into Gien,
continue over the main road and take the smaller D951
heading through water meadows towards

Poilly lez Gien 125m (798/573)
No facilities.

The road is straight and level now as it passes through highly productive farmland running parallel with the River Loire, 1km away to the right.

St. Gondon 133m (804/567)
Gîte d'étape, post office and bar

is soon passed and then, in quick succession, **Lion en Suillias** and **St. Aignan le Jaillard** before the road reaches the outskirts of

*The château
of Sully sur Loire*

Sully sur Loire 128m (825/546)
All facilities including information.
A strange little town, Sully is dominated by its huge 14th-century château with four famous pepper-pot towers rising out of a moat. It was twice visited by Joan of Arc, and you should not miss visiting it if only to marvel at the magnificent chestnut timber work which is to be found in one of the roofs.

The restaurants and bars in Sully are expensive and its tourist office is quite palatial, yet the outskirts of the town look ill kept. Perhaps it has never fully recovered from the bombardment it received during the Second World War.

Leave the town by crossing the bridge over the Loire. There are awkward junctions at both ends of this bridge, and great care should be taken as this is a particularly busy road, especially in high season when coaches clog the roads.

From this point onwards, traces of the Loire Cycle Way are found. The route is not continuous, is badly signed and its sole intention seems to be to keep cyclists off any tarmac road, no matter how far away from the route it takes you. The best advice is to ignore it unless its destination is well signed and obvious.

The D60 from Sully to **St. Benoît** is a well-surfaced quiet road running in a wide sweep along the levée of the Loire. Keep on it and do not follow signs inviting you to follow the cycle-way. Soon the distinct outline of St. Benoît Abbey is seen and the road leads precisely to the square outside it.

St. Benoît sur Loire 111m (833/538)
All facilities including information.
The lovely old town has grown up around the abbey after which it takes its name. It has a couple of peaceful squares and an ancient quay on the banks of the Loire. Its real gem, however, is the great Abbey of St. Benoît itself, said to be one of the holiest places of Christianity.

The abbey is entered through an incredible 11th-century square portal whose capitals are decorated with delightful intricate carvings taken from the New Testament. The floor of the choir is covered in fine mosaics, and hereabouts can be found the burial place of the Capetian king Philippe I. In the crypt are the remains of Saint Benoît, who instigated the Benedictine order of monks and is often known as the patron saint of the west. The abbey has stood here since the 11th century and is a working monastery. Monks serve in the shop, and the Gregorian Chant is sung every Sunday. Finally, do not fail to visit the north portal, with its striking statuary.

Angel and the Devil fight for the soul of man at St. Benoît

STAGE 16

St. Benoît sur Loire to
St. Ay sur Loire (59km) – Total 892km

Route	This uses parts of the Loire Cycleway, keeping close to the banks of the Loire – it is flat, easy riding
Surfaces	Good to Châteauneuf sur Loire, poor between there and Orléans, and very difficult in places beyond Orléans
See	The ancient church at St. Germigny, Orléans Cathedral
Warning	The entrance to Orléans can be extremely busy and dangerous – having crossed the Loire, it may be better to dismount in order to cross the main traffic flow

Ignore the Val de Loire Cycleway signs and exit St. Benoît in a north-westerly direction by a quiet country road, the D60. It wends its way through farmland until it reaches the hamlet of

Germigny des Prés 126m (839/532)

Bars, restaurant.

Here is hidden one of the oldest and most unusual churches in France. Although heavily restored, it was first built by Bishop Théodulfe, a great friend of Charlemagne, in the year 806AD. It is built in the shape of a Greek cross, with a fine cupola at its centre. It has a magnificent apse, which is decorated with 130,000 mosaic cubes depicting two archangels, two cherubs and the Hand of God forming the Arch of Alliance. It was heavily restored in 1868. A visit to this church is one of the high points of the whole journey and should not be missed. The church, which is not well signed, is to be found just off the D60 where it turns a sharp left-hand bend in the centre of the village.

Return to the D60 and ride until modern suburbs are reached. This is the entrance to

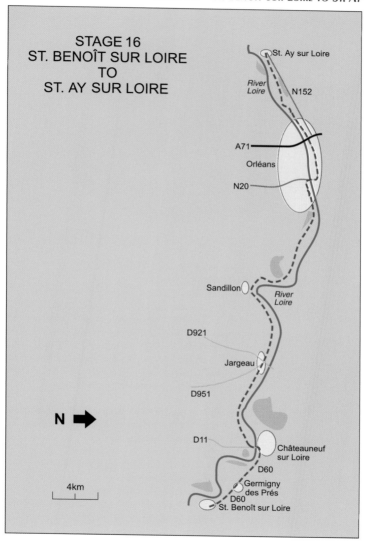

STAGE 16
ST. BENOÎT SUR LOIRE
TO
ST. AY SUR LOIRE

St. Ay sur Loire

River Loire   N152

A71

Orléans

N20

Sandillon   *River Loire*

D921

Jargeau

D951

N ➡

D11

Châteauneuf sur Loire

D60

4km

Germigny des Prés

D60

St. Benoît sur Loire

The mosaic apse of
Germigny des Prés

Châteauneuf sur Loire 112m (844/527)
All facilities including information.

A modern town built on the site of an ancient one, Châteauneuf is very attractive. It boasts a riverside promenade, an ancient town square, a fine church and the remains of the château from which it takes its name. Most of the latter now constitutes the town hall. There is also a large and informative Maritime Museum. It is, however, a very busy town, and great care needs to be taken when negotiating its traffic-infested streets by bicycle.

When entering the town look for a left turn signed to the Loire Bridge. This is your exit road, the D11. As soon as the bridge has been crossed, take an un-numbered road to the right. This is signed as the Val de Loire Cycle Way in the direction of Orléans (a blue sign with white lettering) and should be followed.

The surface is generally quite good, much of it being of tarmac, and the scenery is pleasant. The cycle-way follows the top of the levée for the majority of the journey to **Orléans**, and places where it leaves the levée are clearly signed. Occasionally signs will be met warning that there is no through road to Orléans, but this refers solely to vehicular traffic and cyclists should ignore them. The route could be very exposed in bad weather.

Jargeau 104m (853/518)
All facilities including information.

Keep the River Loire immediately to your right and wherever possible follow signs for the cycle route to Orléans. A long ride on the levée with excellent views of the river and surrounding countryside now follows. There are numerous resting and picnic places, with the small town of **Sandillon** close by if supplies are needed.

As Orléans is approached, the cycle-way widens until it becomes a suburban road which leads to a large leisure complex and swimming pool on the right. The signing is very confusing here, but try to keep as close to the river as possible until a roadbridge over the Loire is reached. Take great care as you cross the river on this bridge which carries a great deal of traffic, and at the next permissible junction turn left following signs to 'centre ville'.

Orléans 94m (878/493)
All facilities including information.
For its size and importance, Orléans is a rather disappointing city. Rebuilding after the Second World War has left it with a small, rather neglected old quarter and a large, faceless shopping area stretching from the cathedral to the Loire. The whole is hemmed in by busy, fast roads, which make cycling difficult.

The one glorious building in Orléans is the cathedral, built in the Gothic style. Fronted by an enormous square, which allows the magnificent west front to be seen to greatest advantage, the building soars upwards, commanding attention. Its twin towers of unusual design give a fortress-like feel to its roofline.

The interior of the building lacks the magnificence of its exterior. Dark stonework and rather uninspiring stained-glass windows depicting the life of Joan of Arc give an atmosphere of eerie neglect. Nevertheless, it should not be missed under any circumstances.

Return to the river but do not cross it. Instead, turn right and ride along the north bank on an indistinct cycle-way which runs alongside a promenade. This is parallel to the extremely busy N152 signed to **Beaugency**. The cycle-way at this point is, in fact, the GR3, although it appears to be used more by cyclists than walkers.

The surface varies between smooth tarmac and a rocky track, at times difficult to negotiate with a loaded touring bike, but always preferable to the *route nationale* thundering close by to the right. Follow this route, which by-passes all hamlets and villages, until a sign is reached pointing out the Fontaine de Rabelais. At this point take a steep but short track to the right at right angles to the cycle-way. This leads almost immediately into

St. Ay sur Loire 88m (892/479)
Overnight accommodation, camp site, supermarket, post office, restaurants and bars.
A large village straddling the N152, St. Ay sur Loire suffers from very heavy traffic.

The west front of Orléans Cathedral

STAGE 17

St. Ay sur Loire to Blois (65km) – Total 957km

Route	Pleasant, flat riding throughout the stage
Surfaces	Good throughout
See	Church, château and medieval centre of Meung sur Loire, ancient Beaugency, the magnificent Château de Chambord (if time allows) and the many glorious buildings in Blois

Much of the riding on this stage is along main roads. Unfortunately, there is little that can be done to alleviate the problem. Wherever feasible, the Loire Cycle Way is used, but at times this route extends the journey by several kilometres before depositing the unsuspecting cyclist only a few metres further along the main road – a fruitless exercise.

Leave St. Ay sur Loire in a south-westerly direction on the N152. Although it is busy, this road is straight and well surfaced and it is not long before it arrives in

Meung sur Loire 90m (898/473)
All facilities including information.

A lovely and fascinating old town dominated by its ancient château and huge 13th-century church, dedicated to St. Liphard, which was once part of the whole castle complex. Narrow medieval streets wind their way between half-timbered houses. Time seems to have passed the whole place by. Even the riverside park seems other-worldly.

With a sigh of relief, leave the N152 and cross the River Loire on the D18, then take the first road to the right signed as the cycle-way to **Beaugency**. This deserted road wanders through water meadows past tiny farming hamlets until it meets the D19 at a cross-roads. Turn right

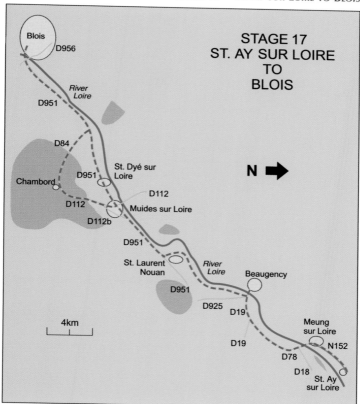

onto this and follow it as it crosses two bridges into the busy town of

Beaugency 86m (913/458)
All facilities including information.
The town is not as pretty as Meung, but it is nevertheless attractive, with cobbled streets, ancient buildings including the Templar House, three curtain walls and seven gates. There is also a large pedestrianised shopping centre

replete with modern sculptures. Other buildings worth seeing include the Château Dunois, which is now a museum, the town hall, the Caesar Tower and the churches of Notre Dame, St. Étienne and Saint Fermin. The 11th-century river bridge with its 22 arches was said to have been built by the devil in a single day! If you feel the urge to replenish supplies, there is a large out-of-town shopping complex on the N152, but this need not be visited.

Instead, re-cross the River Loire and take the first available road to the right, heading for an industrial complex. This is the power station of **St. Laurent des Eaux** and will soon be passed unless a guided visit is required. Afterwards, the country road which has been followed joins the D951 (turn right) at a T-junction. This is a busy, fast road with little means of escape.

Having passed through the hamlet of **Nouan sur Loire**, the next village of any size is

Muides sur Loire 92m (932/439)
Hotel, bar, campsite.
If desired, a road to the left, the D112, can be taken to the Château de Chambord 7km away (this adds 8km to the stage). This is the largest and probably the finest of all Loire châteaux. The grounds are enormous and the château itself is vast. Do not miss walking up and down the double helix staircase, and spend a wonderful hour or two on the roof area surrounded by 365 chimneys, all beautifully decorated.

To return, take the D84 in a north-westerly direction through Montlivault until the D951 is met and joined (turn left).

If a visit to Chambord is not required, continue to follow the D951 towards Blois. Occasionally short stretches of cycle-way appear alongside the road. These are a welcome escape from the traffic but are often in poor condition. Having passed through the village of **St. Dyé sur Loire**, a long, fairly uninteresting stretch of road stays

The huge Château de Chambord

close to the bank of the Loire, sometimes running along its levée. As the city of Blois is approached, a large viaduct crosses the road near to a campsite. Soon afterwards the suburbs of the city line the road.

At the first large roundabout do not cross the river on the fast and dangerous roadbridge but stay on the southern bank of the river as far as the second roadbridge, which is considerably quieter. Ride from here into the centre of the city. Accommodation is expensive and scarce in Blois, and it may be advantageous to find somewhere to stay on the south side of the river before crossing the bridge into

Blois 70m (957/414)
All facilities including information.
Blois is a city steeped in history and intrigue. The magnificent château, which draws admiring visitors from all over the world, can alone detain a visitor for a whole day. The delicate Renaissance architecture and painted ceilings are breathtaking, and the stories of its inhabitants conjure up visions of courtly opulence and wicked revenge.

The Loire, lit by evening sun as it passes through Blois

The cathedral, which is built on the site of a sixth-century chapel dedicated to St. Pierre, is itself dedicated to St. Louis. It is lit by modern stained-glass windows based on calligraphy and is bright and airy, a perfect contrast to the gold and burgundy of the château. The streets of the city wind between cathedral, château and church, and are often clogged with vehicular and pedestrian traffic.

There is more to Blois than tourism, however. It is the centre of a large farming community and is also renowned for its chocolate manufacture. Guided tours of the Poulaine chocolate factory can be arranged.

STAGE 18

Blois to Montlouis
sur Loire (68km) – Total 1025km

Route	A couple of gentle climbs after Amboise relieve the monotony of flat riding
Surfaces	Excellent throughout
See	The flower-bedecked village of Candé sur Beuvron, Chaumont Château, Amboise Château, the Clos Luce, the Chanteloup Pagoda, the church of St. Martin le Beau and the vineyards of Montlouis

This stage includes a diversion from the banks of the Loire to visit a strange monument, vineyards producing some of the finest white wine in the world and a church whose foundations St. Martin may well have visited.

Leave Blois on the D751. This is a riverside road on the south bank which soon passes beneath an AutoRoute standard road which is about to cross the river. Stay on the south bank for another 3km until the road swings sharply to the left, away from the Loire. At this point take a right fork. This minor road continues to hug the river bank and is signed as the cycle-way to

Candé sur Beuvron 70m (975/396)
Gîte d'étape, shop and bar.
The town, which seems to be covered in flowers, sits, as its name implies, on the River Beuvron, a tributary of the Loire. There is an air of bucolic tranquillity about the place after the hectic bustle of Blois.

Having turned right onto the D751 and crossed the bridge, do **not** take the road to the left which is signed as the cycle-way. Instead, stay on the D751, which is a pleasant, quiet, shorter and much less hilly alternative. Having passed through shady woodlands, the road opens out into the village of

The delightful village of Candé sur Beuvron

Chaumont sur Loire 68m (982/389)
Information, garage, bar and shop.
The village, which straddles the main road, has grown up around the Château of Chaumont. The château is approached via a drawbridge and an avenue of trees, providing a superb vista of the countryside hereabouts. The building itself is half castle, half stately house, and was inhabited by some of the greatest players in France's history, including Catherine de Médicis and Diane de Poitiers. The whole château and grounds were extensively restored and refurbished in the 19th century and are certainly worth a visit.

The road, which is rarely very busy, continues through a series of small hamlets. Wine caves begin to appear alongside the road offering tastings. If each were visited, the day's journey would finish long before the next town of importance!

Amboise 60m (1002/369)
All facilities including information.
There is a homely atmosphere about this lovely riverside

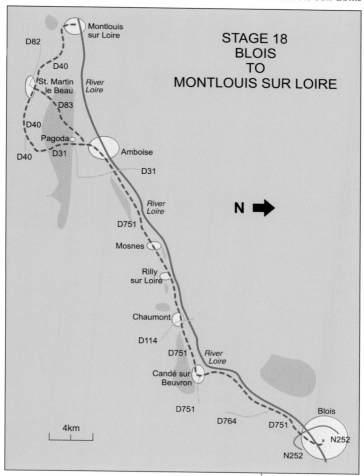

town. It is always busy, but most of its visitors are on foot, having left their vehicular transport parked by the river. They head for three main sites. The Château of Amboise, often altered and extended, is a magnificent building blending Renaissance architecture with Gothic to provide a fortress which demonstrates grace and power combined. As at Chaumont, most of France's great monarchs and historical figures have resided here and had their influence on the place. The interior is still furnished. The Church of St. Denis, dating from 1107, boasts finely carved capitals as well as three Renaissance works, but it is to the Clos Luce that most visitors wend their way. This beautiful brick and stone manor house was the final home of that great European genius Leonardo da Vinci. Apart from being able to visit his apartments, the visitor can marvel at working models made to his original designs.

On leaving the town, return to the D751 and immediately take a left turn (take great care) clearly signed to the **Pagode de Chanteloup** and to **St. Martin le Beau**. This road climbs steeply, crossing a couple of major roads, until at a strange three-road junction there appears the entrance to the

Chanteloup Pagoda 115m (1009/362)
The beautiful if rather rickety structure stands in the gardens of a once magnificent château that was demolished in the 19th century. To see its slender form reflected in its accompanying lake is to appreciate the true beauty of Renaissance architecture. However, the biggest treat, if you have a head for heights, is the view of the Loire and surrounding countryside from its pinnacle.

Now retrace the route as far as the D83 crossroads. Turn left here and ride through the Forest of Amboise until the road emerges, surrounded by vineyards, on the outskirts of

St. Martin le Beau 91m (1019/352)
All facilities except information.
This small wine town, part of the Montlouis appellation, whose grapes are still all hand picked, has a very ancient church whose foundations may stretch back to the time of St. Martin himself. It has a magnificent Romanesque portal and several items of interest inside.

*The Chanteloup
Pagoda beyond
Amboise*

Take the D40 uphill in a north-westerly direction over
the watershed between the rivers Cher and Loire until
signs lead into the centre of

Montlouis sur Loire 75m (1025/346)
All facilities including information.
The white wine produced here is some of the most
beautiful in France. It is often linked with its larger
neighbour, Vouvray, just across the river, but the wine of
Montlouis has a fruitier edge to it. No one should leave
without a lengthy visit to, at least, the Cave Co-operative
on the D751.

Note For cyclists on a
budget, the chambre
d'hôte at Cangé,
St. Martin le Beau
(Appendix A), may be
a better option than
the hotel or château
at Montlouis.

STAGE 19

Montlouis sur Loire to
Montsoreau (86km) – Total 1111km

Route	This is a long, flat ride with much along the way to admire
Surfaces	Poor between La Riche and Savonnières and also between Villandry and the outskirts of Huismes, but otherwise very good
See	The Cathedral and Tour St. Jacques area of Tours, the petrifying wells at Savonnières, the gardens of Villandry, the whole village and panorama at Candes St. Martin and the château of Montsoreau
Warning	The entrance into Tours can be busy whilst the exit can be very dangerous – be prepared to stop and think before committing yourself on roads from which there is no escape.

Leave Montlouis along the D751 riverside road in a westerly direction. Although this is one of the major routes into the city of Tours and is busy, it does not feel particularly dangerous. The road is wide, visibility is good and there are vestiges of a cycle-way in places. As **Tours** is reached, the left side of the road becomes lined with industrial plant and to the right is the Loire.

Soon the towers of the cathedral come into view, and at traffic lights opposite the Pont de Fil turn left to arrive in the square which stands before it.

Tours 48m (1040/331)
All facilities including information.
The capital of Touraine and arguably the principal city on the Loire, Tours deserves time spending on it. There is so much here to explore and enjoy.

The 15th-century cathedral of St. Gatien, dedicated to the man who introduced the Roman town to Christianity, has an interior equally as fine as its exterior. It is principally a Gothic monument with a finely executed west front. Inside are a number of very early stained-glass windows similar to those found in the cathedral at Chartres.

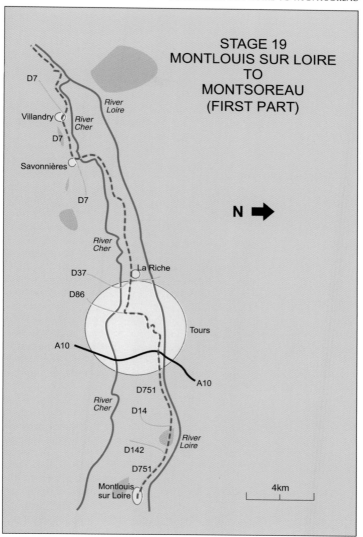

STAGE 19
MONTLOUIS SUR LOIRE
TO
MONTSOREAU
(FIRST PART)

The finest depict the Tree of Jesse and the history of Christianity's greatest saints. There are also two striking rose windows.

To the north side of the cathedral can be found the Psalette, three galleries, a spiral staircase, scriptorium and chapter library all built in the Renaissance style.

The twin towers, 'lacework in stone', are landmarks from miles around, and behind them rises one of the first examples of Gothic architecture at its height, the great apse with its airy buttresses and soaring pillars.

If the narrow streets are followed down to the area round St. Martin's Basilica then much of old Tours will have been visited. The basilica itself and its associated buildings are fascinating, for it was here that St. Martin was buried, his tomb becoming one of the major pilgrimage centres in France. Although much of the mighty original church has disappeared, there is enough remaining to make one realise the importance of St. Martin not just in this region but throughout France. If nothing else, a visit to the crypt in St. Martin's basilica should be made in order to experience the 'holy silence' which pervades the place.

Leaving the city is an arduous task. Ride from the **Basilique Saint Martin** in a southerly direction until the **Boulevard Béranger** is met. Turn right here as far as the **Rue Girardeau**, then turn left along this street until, at a roundabout before crossing the River Cher, you

Flying buttresses on the Cathedral of St. Gatien, Tours

turn right (signed to Villandry and Chinon). Continue along this busy, dangerous road and do not take roads to the left or right which are not for cyclists. Instead continue straight ahead through the village of **La Riche** on a road which suddenly becomes a virtually traffic-free country lane. To the right are market gardens and the railway, to the left appears the River Cher. The road meanders alongside the river past water mills and riverside hamlets before finally reaching a bridge which crosses the Cher, leading into the village of

Savonnières 44m (1053/318)
Bars, shops and restaurants.
The village is well known because of its petrifying wells, in which everyday objects can be placed in the calcium-rich water and 'turned to stone'. The road is lined with riverside bars and restaurants, but there is little else here except a pleasant Romanesque church.

Turn right onto the D7. Pass the petrifying wells, and it is not long before the road becomes lined with parked cars. This is because there is no adequate car park for the famous château and gardens of

Villandry 45m (1057/314)
Hotel, bar, restaurant, information and shop.
It is not surprising that so many people visit Villandry. It is not the château itself which draws the crowds, although it is pleasant enough. The real attraction is the gardens. They are laid out in a series of terraces. Each section is different. There are water gardens, those devoted to love and music, and, most startling of all, a huge kitchen garden inter-planted with both vegetables, flowers and trees bisected by arbours, vines and fountains. The whole garden is a miracle of horticultural devotion dictated by geometric patterning. The most difficult problem is leaving it!

Do not continue along the D7 but take a lane to the right almost opposite the château entrance. This quickly leads

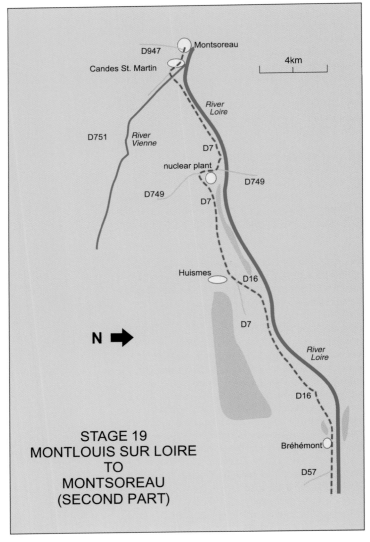

D947
Montsoreau

4km

Candes St. Martin

River Loire

D751

River Vienne

D7

nuclear plant

D749

D749

D7

Huismes

D16

D7

N ➡

River Loire

D16

Bréhémont

D57

STAGE 19
MONTLOUIS SUR LOIRE
TO
MONTSOREAU
(SECOND PART)

The immaculate gardens surrounding Villandry Château

to the south bank of the Loire, which is now followed for many kilometres in a westerly direction.

In the near future a new AutoRoute, the A85, will cross this road, but should not spoil its beauty. This idyllic route feels as though it has been unchanged for centuries – indeed part of it is called the Roman Way. The Loire, having been joined at this point by the River Cher, drifts around sandbanks with an occasional fisherman's craft mirrored on its surface and cottages appear at random, some selling their own home-grown produce. This is truly the Garden of France.

Do not be tempted to turn off this road unless you have a strong desire to visit the rather commercial château of **Ussé**, said to be the setting for *Sleeping Beauty*. Instead, continue heading west until the road swings away from the river and rejoins the D7 just west of **Huismes**.

Turn right onto this road, which will shortly lead to a hideous **nuclear power plant**. In order to avoid passing straight through it, the road turns left and, at a T-junction, turns right and then again left just before the bridge over the Loire. The road is still the D7 and continues to run along the south bank of the River Loire until a bridge is

125

crossed at the confluence of the rivers Vienne and Loire.
From this bridge there is a wonderful view of the pilgrimage town of

Candes St. Martin 75m (1109/262)
Hotel, chambre d'hôte, restaurant, bar and post office.
The village has the honour of possessing one of the most
magnificent churches along the Loire. Built on the site of
the home of St. Martin in the fourth century, this semi-
fortified church is richly decorated both inside and out.
On St. Martin's death, his mortal remains were floated
up-river to be buried at Tours, but this spot was chosen to
build this fine church in his memory. There are the
remains of a château here, but they need not detain the
visitor. However, it is worth struggling up the very steep
hill behind the church to view a magnificent panorama
of the region.

Accommodation is scarce in Candes, but only a couple
of kilometres along the road stands a riverside village
with plenty of reasonably priced hotels and a beautiful
château to visit,

Montsoreau 37m (1111/260)
*Hotels, bars, restaurants, supermarket, shops and
post office.*
The château, now the home of the Goums Museum,
stands – half fortress, half pleasure palace – proudly
above the river with the village clustered round its feet. It
can be very busy in high season.

STAGE 20

Montsoreau to Angers (71km) – Total 1182km

Route	This is a pleasant, flat riverside ride with a few minor undulations after Saumur
Surfaces	Good throughout
See	The château of Saumur and mushroom and wine caves close by, troglodyte dwellings in the cliffs, a series of medieval churches between Saumur and Gennes, Angers château and cathedral as well as numerous beautiful buildings in the city
Warning	The entrance to Angers can be confusing. Cross the motorway and ride parallel to it – do **not** take the slip road onto it

The D947 leads directly from Montsoreau to **Saumur**. This is an excellent if sometimes busy road with much to divert the eye. It follows the south bank of the Loire, with a whole series of wine and mushroom caves vying for attention and custom. It is also interesting to note the number of troglodyte dwellings bordering the road. These have been dug out of the solid limestone which borders the river and are now often occupied by rich Parisians who use them as holiday homes. There are some beautiful views of the river on this stretch of the route, and it is easy to be tempted to stop and admire them before cycling on to

Saumur 34m (1122/249)
All facilities including information.
The capital of the region, Saumur deserves time spending in it. Its white stone buildings give it an air of lightness and its leafy squares tempt visitors to pause and reflect here. The great château, begun in the 14th century but altered several times since, houses two museums – one devoted to the horse, for which Saumur is justly renowned, and a good arts museum including some fine tapestries.

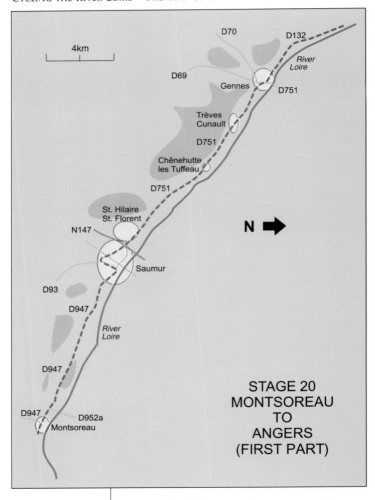

Visits should also be made to the Notre Dame de
Nantilly church, that of St. Pierre and the 16th-century
City Hall. Much of the centre of the city is pedestrianised

Troglodyte dwellings close to Saumur

and the public transport system is excellent. The result is an air of tranquillity which pervades the city. This can be enjoyed even more if the bikes are abandoned for an hour and a tour of the town is made by horse-drawn carriage.

Saumur is also world famous for the sparkling wine produced hereabouts. A visit to a cave, of which there are many in the locality, should not be missed. In fact there are more than 1000km of cellars beneath Saumur.

The route through Saumur is not easy to follow and care should be taken, as it involves wheeling bikes through the pedestrianised area. Turn left at the bridge onto one of the main streets of the city and, on reaching a large roundabout, turn right. Take the next road left and then take a road to the right signed to **Saint Hilaire/Saint Florent**. This town is reached without, apparently, leaving Saumur, as the whole area is built-up.

Saint Hilaire/Saint Florent 30m (1126/245)
All facilities except information.
The town could not, honestly, be described as attractive. It is a township devoted to bottling wines and the road is

129

lined with bottling plants and showrooms designed to tempt the passer-by to taste and purchase crate-loads of the local brew. Cyclists, who can carry little or none at all, are not made to feel so welcome.

The D751, which is quiet, flat and well-surfaced, keeps to the river bank as it passes various visitor attractions mainly concerned with either wine or mushroom production, and the views of the river are excellent. There is an air of affluence about this stretch of the Loire, with luxurious houses and well-tended villages along the route.

Chênehutte–Trèves–Cunault 26m (1134/237)
Gîte d'étape and information.
The villages here straggle along the river bank, but there are two beautiful churches and a fine tower to be visited. The latter, an 11th-century edifice, standing high to the left of the road, marks the route's arrival in the villages. The church of Saint Aubin is as breathtaking as it is surprising. It dates back to the 10th century and contains so much of interest both inside and out that an hour here seems to pass in seconds. Similarly, the fourth-century church of Notre Dame de Cunault is simply beautiful and it is worth spending much time to explore it.

A series of monuments including churches, towers and châteaux line the next section of the D751, enhancing this already picturesque route.

Gennes 26m (1141/230)
All facilities except information.
The sleepy little town has grown up around the only crossing of the Loire between Saumur and Angers. It has a pleasant, shaded park which would make an excellent picnic place, but otherwise it is not a place to detain the cyclist long.

There is an awkward junction in Gennes. Turn right at the T-junction and then take a left turn immediately before the Loire bridge. This is the D132, and from here

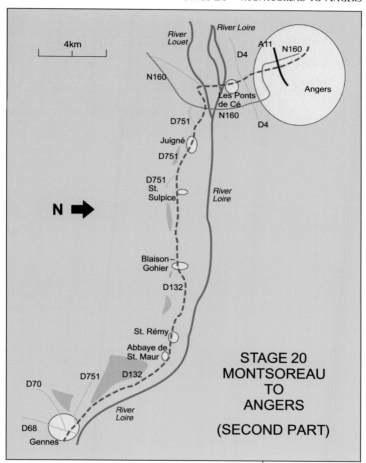

it will be followed for many kilometres. It leads through vineyards and farming country whilst avoiding traffic and townships of any size. Occasionally there are a few small hills to negotiate, but nothing that will cause a problem or even a change of pace!

This region feels as though it has altered little in a thousand years. Buildings are somewhat dilapidated and many monuments are ruined beyond repair. Thus the Gallo-Roman remains and the Abbaye de St. Maur are passed without noticing before entering the wine-producing village of

St. Rémy la Varenne 35m (1152/219)
No facilities.
Explore the 11th-century church after which the village is named. The architecture is stunning, though difficult to take in, owing to the amount of lush foliage in the village.

Vineyards still dominate as the D132 begins to undulate more noticeably. Soon the road swings to the south, away from the river before passing through the twin villages of

Blaison–Gohier 93m (1157/214)
Gîte d'étape.

The road now becomes difficult to follow as a multitude of narrow roads cross and re-cross the route. Pass through **St. Sulpice**, staying on the D132 until the D751 is met at a T-junction in **St. Jean des Mauvrets**. Turn right onto this road as far as **Juigné sur Loire**. Here take the D132 once more as it swings right before passing under the N160, arriving at a T-junction with an unnumbered road. Turn right here towards **Angers** (do **not** turn left for Erigné).
 It should be remembered that Angers is not built on the Loire but on the River Maine, which flows into it further to the west. This necessitates crossing the Loire and then riding several kilometres through suburban sprawl before the centre of the city is reached.
 Having crossed the Loire and passed through the suburb of **St. Aubin**, a very awkward and dangerous junction with the N160 is reached. Take the slip road (to the right) over the latter and then cycle parallel to it (keeping it on your left) on a service road until, at a distinct T-junction, you turn left following signs into the city centre.

Angers 54m (1182/189)

All facilities including information.

Angers is undoubtedly a fine city and time should be spent exploring it. It is dominated by its enormous 13th-century fortress of a château, almost 1km long, which houses the world famous Apocalypse Tapestry. Its formidable, dark walls rise over 50m from its flower-filled moat, and its 17 mighty towers protect it from any assault.

The best part of a day could be spent in the château alone. The tapestry, which is claimed to be the largest in the world, is housed in a specially designed chamber and consists of 70 different scenes produced in the 14th century. It is, without doubt, one of the masterpieces of medieval art.

Modern fountain and sculpture in Angers

Interest in fine arts is well catered for in the city, which has several museums, including that in the St. Jean Hospital (itself worth a visit) with tapestries produced by Jean Lurçat and exhibitions of sculpture. The finest of these is to be found in the David d'Angers Gallery (a beautifully and imaginatively restored church). Here are gathered the entire works of the sculptor David who was born in the town in the 18th century. A combined ticket for entrance to these museums can be obtained, at considerable saving, from any museum.

The cathedral of Saint Maurice, too, demands time spending in it. It has wonderful 12th-century Angevine vaulting and excellent stained glass.

*Inside the David
d'Angers Museum*

Accommodation in the city can be expensive close
to the château and cathedral, but far less expensive
hotels can be found in the vicinity of the bus station.

STAGE 21

Angers to Drain (78km) – Total 1260km

Route	A number of short hills will be encountered throughout this stage with a steep one to finish
Surfaces	Good
See	The panoramas from the Angevine Corniche and Montjean and the ancient centre at Ancenis

In order to leave Angers and regain the route along the Loire, the last 8km of the previous stage must be retraced. This is more difficult than it sounds, as some of the roads are one way, and on reaching the awkward junction with the N160 it is necessary to wheel the bikes over the slip road (which is one way) to regain the safer road into **St. Aubin**. When the River Loire has been re-crossed, ride straight on up the hill into **Erigné** and take the D751 to the right (clearly signed to **Chalonnes sur Loire**) into

Mûrs Erigné 15m (1195/176)
No facilities, although all are available between Angers and this point.

This is a good, quiet road which begins to show signs of some of the hills in store on this surprising stage.

Denée 89m (1200/171)
Bar and post office.

The next section of the route is along the same D751, with occasional glimpses of the widening Loire valley to the right until it reaches

Rochefort sur Loire 50m (1205/166)
Bar, shops and post office.

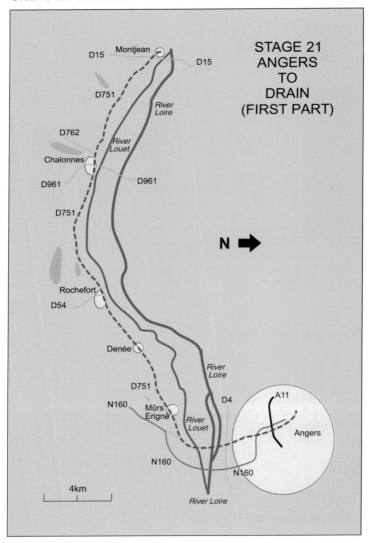

STAGE 21
ANGERS
TO
DRAIN
(FIRST PART)

Montjean
D15
D15
River Loire
D751
D762
River Louet
Chalonnes
D961
D961
D751
N ➡
Rochefort
D54
Denée
River Loire
D751
D4
N160
A11
Mûrs Erigné
River Louet
Angers
N160
N160
River Loire
4km

This ancient robber's hideout has several interesting old houses with turrets and watchtowers. It is famous for its heady Quart de Chaume wine.

The D751 from here is designated the **Angevine Corniche**. For the rest of the stage it climbs and descends regularly, though rarely does it exceed 100m. There are, however, some long, slow ascents and some steep descents, providing a pleasant change after days of flat riding. Consequently, the views improve throughout the stage.

Chalonnes sur Loire 20m (1215/156)
All facilities including gîte d'étape.
Chalonnes, on the southern end of one of the few bridging points of the River Loire in this area, is a busy little town, with most of its shops on the main street, which should be followed to the outskirts of the town where it becomes the D751 once more.

Continue to follow the D751 as it undulates until a long, steady descent leads into the riverside town of

The quiet backwater of Chalonnes sur Loire

137

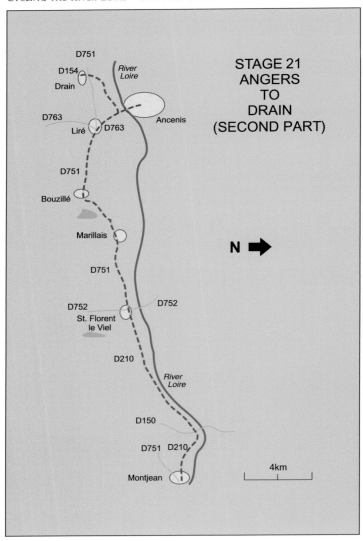

STAGE 21
ANGERS
TO
DRAIN
(SECOND PART)

D751
D154
Drain
River Loire
D763
Liré
D763
Ancenis
D751
Bouzillé
Marillais
N ➡
D751
D752
D752
St. Florent
le Viel
D210
River Loire
D150
D751 D210
Montjean
4km

Montjean sur Loire 16m (1224/147)

All facilities, including information, with good views over the river from the church.

The 'Ecomuseum' has displays relating to the Loire, lime kilns and coal mining as well as hemp working. If you have time, visit the 19th-century barge or even take a trip on the river and hear a fisherman's view of the Loire.

Do not leave Montjean on the D751 which swings south, away from the river into the Angevine country-side, but take the D210 along the southern edge of the river. It is clearly signed along a flat stretch of road to the hilly little town of

St. Florent le Viel 50m (1239/132)

Information, gîte d'étape and shops.

The church dominates this village, which was a centre of fighting in the 18th-century Vendéen War. As well as the abbey church, which features some interesting sculpture, there is also a local history museum and the abbey farm to visit.

Leave the village on the D751 once more. This road again begins to climb until it reaches the hill-top village of

Marillais 60m (1244/127)

Fine church at highest point in village.

The D751 continues to undulate as it passes through

Bouzillé 89m (1247/124)

Gîte d'étape and nearby Château de la Bourgonnière.

The D751 now climbs and descends through rich pas-turelands several kilometres south of the Loire until it reaches a crossroads with the D763 in the village of **Liré**. Turn right onto this road and descend to the bridge over the River Loire which leads into the centre of

Ancenis 22m (1255/116)
All facilities including information (accommodation is very scarce).

An attractive riverside wine town famous for its Muscadet white wines, it can be very busy in high season, with a small ancient quarter boasting restaurants and bars close to its ruined château and ramparts. The 15th-century church of St. Pierre boasts a rare steeple door and there is an old Ursuline convent to visit. There is also a pleasant park, the Eperon Garden. Ancenis Castle, which at present is closed for restoration work, was a Breton frontier stronghold and has fine circular towers.

Re-cross the Loire by the bridge and immediately take a right turn next to a restaurant onto an unnumbered road close to the south bank of the river. Follow this until, once more, it meets the D751 at a T-junction, and cross it at a 'dog-leg' to climb steeply into the hill-top village of

Drain 70m (1260/111)
Chambre d'hôte, campsite, artificial lake, restaurant, church and shops.

STAGE 22
Drain to Savenay (81km) – Total 1341km

Route	An easy, flat ride with some confusing route-finding beyond Coueron
Surfaces	Generally good but could be rough between Thouaré and Nantes on the GR3 (road-side cycle lanes through centre of Nantes)
See	Ancient village of Champtoceaux, Nantes cathedral, the Audubon Marais and the lake and woodland south-east of Savenay
Warning	Avoid major roads entering Nantes – they are too dangerous for cyclists

The smiling Loire has a sting in its tail. As the end of the journey is approached, a stage which begins with a whole series of short, steep hills ends with one of the most monotonous, flat rides of the whole tour. You have been warned!

Drain is left by descending the steep hill climbed the previous evening until the D751 is reached. Turn left onto it at this busy junction and negotiate a series of short but steep hills which eventually lead into the picturesque country town of

Champtoceaux 52m (1266/105)
All facilities including information.
By-passed by the main road, this is a most attractive township with an ancient church containing 19th-century stained glass and citadel ruins overlooking the Loire. The finest panorama of the Loire, however, is to be found in the Cédraie Park.

Regain the D751 and descend with fine views of **Oudon** and its ancient castle over on the far side of the river. Do not cross the bridge into this town, however, but keep to the increasingly hilly D751. This road winds away from the river until it climbs back to a vantage point over the Loire at the town of

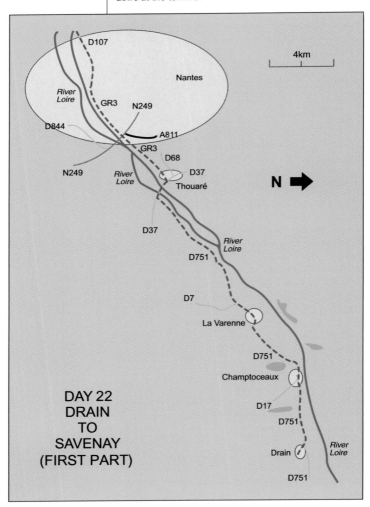

Entrance to the Citadel at Champtoceaux

La Varenne 60m (1271/100)
All facilities except information.

Having left the town by a steep descent, turn right at a distinct T-junction onto the road which is still designated the D751. Do **not** go ahead on the D7.

This road now follows closely the south bank of the Loire, which is dotted with islands and huge sandbanks. There are numerous hamlets along this stretch of the river offering food, drinks, accommodation and sailing trips along the Loire. Nevertheless, this road does not appear to be busy and, provided there is no headwind, this is a charming stretch of the river.

After about 10km, look for a roadbridge spanning the Loire. It leaves the south bank at a crossroads with the D37. Turn right onto the bridge and ride over the Loire and the Ile de la Chênaie before arriving at the outskirts of **Thouaré sur Loire**. There is no need to ride into this small town unless provisions are needed. Instead, take a track down to the north bank of the river, where the GR3 long-distance footpath is encountered. Although this is officially for pedestrians, it is obvious that many cyclists use it to avoid the nightmare which is the approach by road into **Nantes**.

Turn right onto the GR3 and follow it alongside the north bank of the river in a westerly direction. Pass beneath the N249 and follow the track as it widens and then becomes a tarmac road which leads into the very heart of

Nantes 25m (1298/73)
All facilities including information.

Nantes is an enormous city centering on the point where the River Erdre enters the River Loire. It has both commercial areas and heavy industry as well as a small ancient quarter close to the Place Royal. Consequently, it is an exceptionally busy city to ride in, and cyclists need to take every care when leaving cycle lanes or crossing junctions. The cathedral is, at present, undergoing major structural repair following a fire in 1972 and is closed to the public, but one can still visit the Chapel of St. Étienne, the Japanese Garden and the Château of the Dukes of Brittany.

As soon as the GR3 has been left behind, a clear cycleway, marked on the road in green, follows the north bank of the Loire through the city. This runs alongside the D107, which is signed for **Coueron** and should not be left. At times it looks very unpromising as it heads through dockland and heavy industrial plants whilst passing beneath the breathtaking bridge which carries the ring road over the Loire.

Finally, the urban sprawl of Nantes shows signs of coming to an end as the road enters the rather down-at-heel town of

Coueron 17m (1313/58)
Shops, bars and vast gypsy encampment.

The exit from the town is difficult to find. Take the road (no number) which follows the north bank of the river until it runs into a small estate of bungalows. A road leading north-west from here is signed to the Audubon Marais. This is a vast area of reclaimed marshland criss-crossed with canals and drainage dykes. It is perfectly

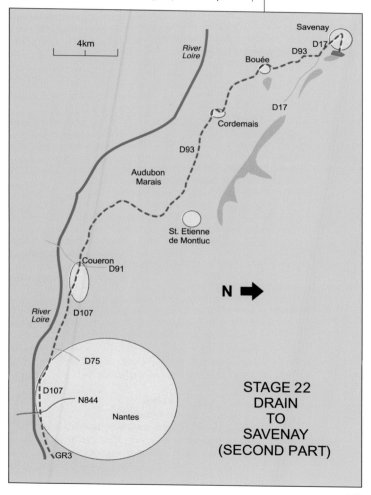

STAGE 22
DRAIN
TO
SAVENAY
(SECOND PART)

flat and there are few landmarks. Unfortunately there are few, if any, road signs either, and map and compass may be needed to navigate through the vast cobweb of unmarked lanes. Even the hamlets are unnamed. There is little of interest to divert the eye and the riding becomes tedious.

Your goal is the village of **Cordemais**. There is a landmark here, as it is the home of yet another nuclear power station, and its tall towers and chimneys can be seen from afar. Ride into the centre of the village, and at the junction in its centre take the D93. This will lead into the little village of

Sluice gates in the Audubon Marais

Bouée 11m (1335/36)
No facilities.

Pass through the village on the D93 and follow it until it reaches a T-junction with the D17. Turn left onto this busy road and within a couple of kilometres climb the steep hill to the centre of the railway town of

Savenay 65m (1341/30)
All facilities except information.
Only a 1km climb from the town centre is a most attractive lake surrounded by trees. Here can be found many leisure pursuits as well as an excellent restaurant and small hotel.

STAGE 23

Savenay to St. Nazaire (30km) – Total 1371km

Route	A short, easy, flat stage to finish the tour with plenty of time to organise transport home
Surfaces	Generally good, but rough between Savenay and Donges and also around the docks in St. Nazaire
See	Port et Base sous-Marine in St. Nazaire
Warning	The entrance into St. Nazaire can be confusing – cross the D213, but do **not** take it

Return down the hill from the centre of Savenay to the junction with the D17. This time do not turn onto this road but cross it onto a minor road which immediately crosses the railway line. As soon as the railway has been crossed, turn right along a lane which runs parallel and south of the railway. Follow this past the station until the N171 (looking like a motorway) can be seen ahead. Do not join this but swing left, staying on the lane which now runs parallel to both the N171 and the railway line.

When the railway has been crossed at an unmanned crossing, turn left at the next crossroads onto the D100. This is a good road passing through the last piece of countryside to be found before arriving in **St. Nazaire**. Unfortunately, the road can be busy with oil tankers leaving the huge refinery which now looms on the left. Stay on the D100 into the centre of

Donges 5m (1352/19)
All facilities except information.

The D100 virtually by-passes Donges, but it is safer for cyclists to ride through the town and join the D100 1km further down the road. Traffic can now be very heavy.

On arriving at a T-junction, turn left, almost back on oneself, onto a road still designated the D100 with a

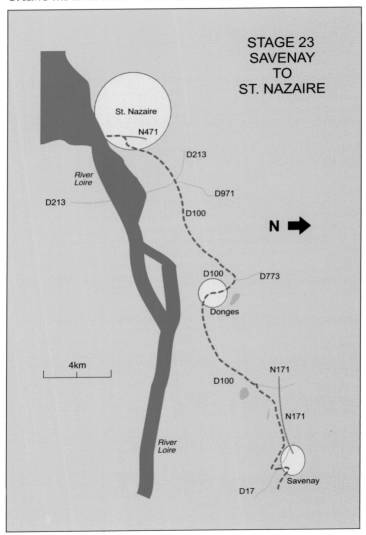

STAGE 23
SAVENAY
TO
ST. NAZAIRE

St. Nazaire

N471

D213

River
Loire

D971

D213

D100

N

D100

D773

Donges

N171

D100

N171

River
Loire

4km

Savenay

D17

poorly maintained cycle track offering little protection from the constant traffic.

Having passed the airport, the road reaches an extremely complicated multiple roundabout close to the end of the astounding Pont de St. Nazaire, truly a bridge through the sky. (It is said that cyclists may use it, but only those wishing to visit heaven very quickly will try!) It is worth dismounting here and examining the road lay-out very carefully; if necessary, do a circuit of the round-about to ascertain where each exit leads. The signs are confusing. Do **not** go onto the D213, as this is too dangerous. Instead look for signs to the port and follow these as they lead through the docks. Once past here, follow signs for the town centre and then the shore.

On reaching the American Monument there, dip your wheels in the Atlantic, and the cycle route from the source to the mouth of the River Loire has been achieved.

St. Nazaire 0m (1371/0)
All facilities including information.
The approach to St. Nazaire can be extremely off-put-ting, but the town itself has a wealth of interesting places to visit. The modernistic town centre invites exploration, with plenty of reasonably priced accommodation.

The shipyards at St. Nazaire

The old quarter near to the shore is fascinating, as is the new shipbuilding yard where vast cruise liners are constructed. The place which draws most visitors is the site of the 'indestructible' German submarine pens – colossal reinforced concrete buildings constructed to protect German U-boats from Allied bombing during the Second World War. Here a huge museum leads the visitor through the story of St. Nazaire's part in the Second World War and the story of the mighty trans-Atlantic liners which were constructed here.

Being on the Atlantic coast, St. Nazaire boasts 20 beaches and yachting marinas full of pleasure craft. It was once the chief port for passage to South America, and before the Second World War it had a thriving commercial heart. The construction of the German submarine pens ended that by creating a target for massive allied bombing raids which destroyed the city, if not the pens. Gradually, the place is being sensitively rebuilt, becoming the ideal place to end this journey along the mighty waterway, the River Loire.

Arrival at the American Monument in St. Nazaire

Trains from St. Nazaire to the Channel coast for return to England leave daily.

BIBLIOGRAPHY

John Ardagh, *The Book of France*, Leicester: W. H. Smith. 1980
ISBN – 0 7112 0059 9
A large, comprehensive reference book looking at numerous aspects of French life region by region. The Loire Valley is dealt with specifically.

John Ardagh, *Rural France*, London: Century. 1983
Provides a real insight into French country life, which is now, sadly, disappearing. There is an excellent section on the Loire Valley and its source in the Auvergne.

Rebecca King, *Illustrated Guide to France*, Basingstoke: Automobile Association. 1992
Although this is principally intended for motorists, it provides a great deal of background information in preparation for this cycle tour. It is clearly set out and easy to digest.

Michael Busselle, *Discovering the Villages of France*, London: Pavilion Books. 1991
An interesting section on southern France includes locations along the Ardèche and Volane valleys.

Michelin, *Provence*, Harrow: Michelin. Regularly updated
ISBN – 2 06 013 642-3
The most detailed tourist guide to the start of this journey. Small enough to carry with you.

Kate Baillie, *Provence & the Côte d'Azure – The Rough Guide*, London: Rough Guides. 1996
ISBN – 1-85828-127-X
A simple if rather heavy guide to the first few stages of the journey, with the emphasis on cheap and cheerful. Straightforward, uncluttered writing.

Sara Midda, *Sketchbook from Southern France*, London: Sidgwick & Jackson. 1990
ISBN – 0-283-06050-6
The perfect bedtime book to give the 'feel' of southern France before you leave on this journey.

A.N. Brangham, History, *People and Places in Auvergne*, Bourne End: Spurbooks. 1977
ISBN – 0 904978 63 X
Still one of the most detailed books about the area through which the first part of this journey is made.

Michelin, *Châteaux of the Loire*, London: Michelin. Regularly updated
ISBN – 2 06 013 211-8
The definitive guide to the Loire Valley from Sancerre to Nantes. Its architectural notes are unsurpassed.

Paul Robert-Houdin, *La Féerie Nocturne des Châteaux de la Loire*, France: Libraire Hachette. 1958
It is worth struggling with the French to appreciate this handbook. Some remarkable black and white photographs.

André Bourin, *The Châteaux of the Loire*, Paris: Editions Sun Paris. 1977
A concise description of all the châteaux of the Loire worth noting in alphabetical order. Stunning photographs plus information on Son et Lumière displays.

A & S Mouraret, *Gîtes d'étape Refuges, France et Frontières*, Vélizy: Guides La Cadole. 1996 (regularly updated)
ISBN – 2-908567-06-7
One of the foremost independent guides of where to stay cheaply in France. Always worth carrying despite its weight.

Clotilde Mallard, *Gîtes d'étape & de Séjour*, Paris: Gîtes de France. Annually updated
ISBN – 2-907071-80-7
Extremely comprehensive guide to cheap accommodation in France. Always telephone ahead if using this guide.

Julian Worthington, *The Vineyards of France*, Dorking: Templar Books. 1994
ISBN – 1-85962-005-1
Too big to carry on a bike, but excellent for those dark winter evenings when planning the journey. Use this book and you won't miss many of the great vineyards along the route.

MAPS

IGN *No. 59 Privas Ales*, Institut Geographique National Serie Verte 1:100,000
ISBN – 2-11100-591-6

IGN *No. 50 St Étienne Le Puy en Velay*, Institut Geographique National Serie Verte 1:100,000 ISBN – 2-11000-507-6

IGN *No. 43 Lyon Vichy*, Institut Geographique National Serie Verte 1:100,000

IGN *No. 36 Nevers Autun*, Institut Geographique National Serie Verte 1:100,000
ISBN – 2-11000-368-5

IGN *No. 27 Orléans La Charité sur Loire*, Institut Geographique National Serie Verte 1:100,000 ISBN – 2-11000-276-X

IGN *No. 26 Orléans Tours*, Institut Geographique National Serie Verte 1:100,000

IGN *No. 25 Angers Chinon*, Institut Geographique National Serie Verte 1:100,000

IGN *No. 24 Nantes Châteaubriant*, Institut Geographique National Serie Verte 1:100,000

APPENDIX A
Accommodation and Information

Orange
Tourist Info – Tel: 04 90 34 70 88/33

Châteauneuf du Pape
Tourist Info – Tel: 04 90 83 71 08

Chambre d'hôte
M. & Mme Melchor
La Font du Pape
84230 Châteauneuf du Pape
Tel: 04 90 83 73 97

Saint Martin d'Ardèche
Tourist Info – Tel: 04 75 98 70 91

Hotel Les Mimosas
Rue du Candelas,
07700 Saint Martin d'Ardèche
Tel: 04 75 04 62 79

Vallon
Tourist Info – Tel: 04 75 88 04 01
www.vallon-pont-darc.com

Gîte d'étape
Escapade Loisirs
Place de la Mairie
07150 Vallon
Tel: 04 75 88 07 87

Les Mazes
Chambre d'hôte
Jean Pierre Helly
Les Mazes
07150 Vallon
Tel: 04 75 37 18 44

Vals les Bains
Tourist Info – Tel: 04 75 37 49 27
www.vals-les-bains.com

Hotel de l'Europe
86, Rue Jean Jaurès
07600 Vals les Bains
Tel: 04 75 37 43 94

Le Gerbier de Jonc –
Gîte d'étape
c/o C & G Breysse
07510 Ste Eulalie
Tel: 04 75 38 81 51

Goudet –
Gîte d'étape
c/o Ferme Auberge du Pipet
43150 Goudet
Tel: 04 71 57 18 05

Le Puy en Velay –
Tourist Info – Tel: 04 71 09 38 41
www.ot-lepuyenvelay.fr

Gîte d'étape
Centre d'hébergement Pierre
Cardinal,
Rue Jules-Vallès
43000 Le Puy en Velay
Tel: 04 71 05 52 40
or
Hôtel Saint Jacques
7, Place Cadelade
43000 Le Puy en Velay
Tel: 04 71 07 20 40

Aurec sur Loire
Tourist Info – Tel: 04 77 35 42 65

Le Pertuiset
Hôtel le Pertuiset *(closed for
renovation in July 2008)*
50, Rue Roger Salengro
42240 Unieux
Tel: 04 77 35 75 63

Neulise
Chambre d'hôte
M. La Chaize
Neulise

St. Jodard
Chambre d'hôte
Philippe and Claudie Durel
Chez Daguet
St. Jodard
Tel: 04 77 63 45 34
Email: durel.philippe@wanadoo.fr

Roanne
Tourist Info – Tel: 04 77 71 51 77

Marcigny
Tourist Info – Tel: 03 85 25 39 06

Chambre d'hôte
M. & Mme. Ricol
La Musardière
50, Rue de la Tour
71110 Marcigny
Tel: 03 85 25 38 54

Gannay sur Loire –
Chambre d'hôte
Peter & Trudi de Lange
Domaine du Bourg
03230 Gannay sur Loire
Tel: 04 70 43 49 01

Nevers
Tourist Info – Tel: 03 86 68 46 00
www.ville-nevers.fr

Hôtel de Verdun
4, Rue de Lourdes
58000 Nevers
Tel: 03 86 61 30 07

Sancerre
Tourist Info – Tel: 02 48 54 08 21
www.sancerre.net/otsi

Hotel Saint Martin
Rue Saint Martin
18300 Sancerre
Tel: 02 48 54 21 11

Briare le Canal
Tourist Info – Tel: 02 38 31 24 51

Hôtel le Cerf
Boulevard Buyser
45250 Briare le Canal
Tel: 02 38 37 00 80

Saint Benoît sur Loire
Tourist Info – Tel: 02 38 35 79 00

Chambre d'hôte
M & Mme L. Leclerc,
21, Route de Sully
Fleury 45730
St. Benoît-sur-Loire
Tel: 02 38 35 10 80
or
Hotel de la Madelaine
65, Rue Orléanaise
45730 Saint Benoît sur Loire
Tel: 02 38 35 71 15

Orléans
Tourist Info – Tel: 02 38 24 05 05

St. Ay sur Loire
Hotel L'Orangerie
RN 152
45130 St. Ay sur Loire
Tel: 02 38 88 84 57

Blois
Tourist Info – Tel: 02 54 90 41 41

Hotel Le Pavillon
2, Avenue Wilson
41000 Blois
Tel: 02 54 74 23 27

Amboise
Tourist Info – Tel: 02 47 57 09 28
www.amboise-valdeloire.com

Saint Martin le Beau
Chambre d'hôte
M. & Mme. Moyer
Domaine Aurore de Beaufort
23, Rue des caves 'Cangé'
37270 Saint Martin le Beau
Tel: 02 47 50 61 51

Tours
Tourist Info – Tel: 02 47 05 58 08

Montsoreau
Hotel La Loire
D 947
49730 Montsoreau
Tel: 02 41 51 70 06

Saumur
Tourist Info – Tel: 02 41 40 20 60
www.saumur-tourisme.com

Angers
Tourist Info – Tel: 02 41 23 50 00

Hôtel des Négotiants
11, Place Molière
49100 Angers
Tel: 02 41 88 24 08

Drain (Nr. Ancenis)
Ancenis Tourist Info –
Tel: 02 40 83 07 44

Chambre d'hôte
Clos Saint Martin
9, Rue des Mauges
49530 Drain (Ancenis)
Tel: 02 40 98 29 71

Savenay
Hôtel Le Relais du Lac
J. Mathieu
44260 Savenay
Tel: 02 40 58 82 93

Saint Nazaire
Tourist Info – Tel: 02 40 91 76 84

Hotel Le Maine
23, Rue du Maine
44600 Saint Nazaire
Tel: 02 40 22 52 23

APPENDIX B
Full Kit List

Bicycle lights
Folding spare tyre
Water bottles
Cycle computer
Cycle locks
Cycling gloves
Helmets
Plastic tape
Tools
Spare spokes
Puncture repair outfit
Spare inner tubes
Pump
Velcro straps

Dog-dazer
Mini electric kettle +
EEC adaptor
Mending kit
First aid kit
Insect repellant
Army knife
Scissors
Lighter
Tissues
Polythene bags

Cutlery
Plates

Cups
Dishcloth
Pan scourer
Universal plug
Stretch washing line
Washing-up liquid
Clothes washing liquid
Mini cool bag
Maps and compass
Guides
Dictionary
Camera
Films
Mini binoculars
Dictaphone

Passport
E111
Currency
Credit cards
Debit cards

Spectacles
Sun glasses
Pen & pencil
Notebook
Toothbrush
Tooth gel
Shower gel

Fibre towels
Toilet roll
Sun cream
Lip salve

Clothes
Thermals
Pertex jackets
Waterproof clothing
Padded shorts
Spare shoes
Sleeping bags
Pocket pillows
Food
Glucose tablets
Isostar sachets
Coffee
Dried milk
Sugar cubes
Emergency dried meal

APPENDIX C
Useful Addresses

Cyclist Touring Club
Cotterell House
69, Meadrow, Godalming
Surrey GU7 3HS
Tel: 01483 417217
www.ctc.org.uk

Camping Equipment & Clothing
Cotswold, 42–46 Uxbridge Rd
Shepherd's Bush
London W12 8ND
Tel: 0181 743 2976
www.cotswold-outdoor.co.uk

**Comité Régional du
Tourisme des Pays de la Loire**
2, Rue de la Loire – BP20411
F-44204 Nantes cedex 2
Tel: 0033 240 48 24 20

Coolmax Socks
Ridgeview Inc.
P.O. Box 8
N.C. 28658
USA
Tel: 001 704 464 2972

Dog-Dazer
Richard Wiley
43, Northcote Road
London SW11 1YY
Tel: 0171 228 2360

European Bike Express
31, Baker Street
Middlesbrough
Cleveland TS1 2LF
Tel: 01642 251440
www.bike-express.co.uk

French National Tourist Office
178, Piccadilly
London W1J 9AL
Tel: 09068 244 123

Gîtes de France
Maison de Gîtes de France & du
    Tourisme Vert
Métro Trinité
59, Rue Saint Lazare
75439 Paris Cedex 09
Tel: 01 49 70 75 75

Ortlieb Bags
Lyon Equipment
Rise Hill Mill
Dent
Sedbergh
Cumbria LA10 5QL
Tel: 01539 625 493
www.ortlieb.de

Stanford's Map Shop
12, Long Acre
Covent Garden
London WC2
Tel: 0171 836 1321

Trek Cycles USA
15, Old Bridge Way
Shefford
Bedfordshire SG17 5HQ
Tel: 01462 811 458
www.trekbikes.com

APPENDIX D

Glossary of Terms (English–French)

accident	**un accident**	main road	**une route**
		map	**une carte**
bakery	**une boulangerie**	money	**l'argent**
bicycle	**un velo/**	motorway	**une AutoRoute**
	une bicyclette		
bottle	**une bouteille**	nut	**un écrou**
brake	**un frein (n)**		
	freiner (v)	oil	**la huile**
bread	**le pain**		
break	**casser (v)**	pedal	**une pédale**
bridge	**un pont**	pump	**une pompe**
bus station	**la gare routière**	puncture	**une crevaison**
cable	**un câble**	railway	**un chemin de fer**
castle	**un château**	railway station	**la gare**
chain	**une chaîne**	river	**une rivière**
change	**la monnaie**	room	**une chambre**
church	**une église**		
city	**une cité**	saddle	**une selle**
		spanner	**une clé à écrous**
direction	**une direction**	spoke	**un rayon**
door	**une porte**	square	**une place**
a drink	**un boisson**	street	**une rue**
		supermarket	**un hypermarché**
field	**un champ**		
		town hall	**L'hotel de ville/**
garage	**un garage**		**La Mairie**
gear	**une vitesse**	tyre	**un pneu**
grease	**la graisse**	water	**l'eau**
		wheel	**une roue**
handlebars	**le guidon**		
helmet	**un casque**		
house	**une maison**		

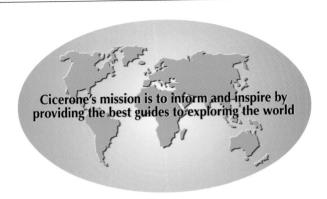

Cicerone's mission is to inform and inspire by providing the best guides to exploring the world

Since its foundation 40 years ago, Cicerone has specialised in publishing guidebooks and has built a reputation for quality and reliability. It now publishes nearly 300 guides to the major destinations for outdoor enthusiasts, including Europe, UK and the rest of the world.

Written by leading and committed specialists, Cicerone guides are recognised as the most authoritative. They are full of information, maps and illustrations so that the user can plan and complete a successful and safe trip or expedition – be it a long face climb, a walk over Lakeland fells, a Himalayan traverse, an alpine cycle tour or a ramble in the countryside.

With a thorough introduction to assist planning, clear diagrams, maps and colour photographs to illustrate the terrain and route, and accurate and detailed text, Cicerone guides are designed for ease of use and access to the information.

If the facts on the ground change, or there is any aspect of a guide that you think we can improve, we will always be delighted to hear from you.

Cicerone Press
2 Police Square Milnthorpe Cumbria LA7 7PY
Tel: 015395 62069   Fax: 015395 63417
info@cicerone.co.uk   www.cicerone.co.uk